A Thankful Journey With The Lord

The Years I Never Wanted To Go Through...

Susi Lorett

A Thankful Journey with the Lord

©2017 Susi Lorett

All rights reserved. No part of this book may be reproduced in any manner without written permission from the author. For information, please contact the author.

Printed and bound in the United States

ISBN-13: 978-1548694647

ISBN-10: 1548694649

For information contact Susi Lorett at honeybearhouse2015@gmail.com

*Scripture quotations taken from
the New American Standard Bible (NASB),
Copyright 1960, 1962, 1963, 1968, 1971, 1972, 1973, 1975, 1977, 1995
by the Lockman Foundation. Used by permission. www.Lockman.org*

Dedication

I am totally indebted and completely grateful for my "great cloud of witnesses".

So many friends and family members have prayed for me.

You have all walked alongside me on this journey.

You have felt the pain with me and shared the joy.

I could never list you all

and so I am truly Thankful that the Lord has seen each one!!

Thank You, Lord, for Your people!

Foreword

It seems at every turn lives are imploding on multiple levels, especially in marriages. We are like "Alice in Wonderland" falling down the rabbit hole only to become ensnared in a web of adversity leading to darkness and confusion.

This is a devotional that holds the keys to unlocking the doors within adversity. Keys that open treasures to victory, peace with the storm, and the knowing there is a living God with real answers to lives trapped in the maze of adversity. This devotional is unlike any you have ever read. It takes you through the journey of Susi Lorett's 18 year marriage unexpectedly tumbling down the rabbit hole only to discover, once hitting bottom, the greatest treasure of all.

This is a devotional where God took an ordinary life, imploding from the inside out, and made it extraordinary. This is God's story.

Kitty Ramirez, Training Director

His Truth Transforms International

5745 132nd Street

Oklahoma City, OK 73142

405-603-2020

www.Histruthtransforms.org

Prologue

This is my story, the story of how God set my feet on this journey without me even realizing. I'm surprised by what He has done!

> *"For whoever wishes to save his life shall lose it;*
> *but whoever loses his life for My sake shall find it."*
>
> *--Matthew 16:25*

The 7 Rules, Thank You, Lord

In the beginning of this journey, I had these 7 Rules coming across my mind. At first, they sounded like - #2 "Don't believe anything "he" says". But as time went on, the Lord brought His truth up against the Rules, adding a fresh layer –so now, Rule #2 looks like this:

Rule #2   Don't dialogue with the devil. God is truth!

In fact, the Lord transformed my thoughts with His truth. Thank You, Lord, for meeting me here, and there and everywhere I am, AND for transforming me into Your Glory, day by day.

You'll find the 7 Rules scattered about, along with some things I've been through on my Journey through divorce. Added in is God's word which He's brought to me along the way. The pages are not in any particular order but are dated to give the reader an idea of the passing of time. I've prayed for you each time I write—that He will meet you and you will be changed forever by knowing Him more! Here's a list of the 7 Rules for you to ponder God's goodness as you go!

Rule #1 Don't try to figure it out…it could hurt your brain. God knows!

Rule #2 Don't dialogue with the devil. God is truth!

Rule #3 No one gets to say who I am but God. God says!!

Rule #4 God will show you what you need to see. God sees!

Rule #5 God's time is perfect. God endures!

Rule #6 Lay down the *why*. God understands!

Rule #7 God's arm is long enough to walk with me every step. God loves!

Rule #8 God, indeed, has more power than everyone or everything. God is!

It was in the days leading up to the Pre-trial and Trial that the Lord brought me Rule #8. This last rule was spoken to my heart during that time when I was really, truly afraid of losing even more than I already had. I got a glimpse of what God might do! Thank You, Lord, for speaking to me again! Halleluiah!!

Just a note: When I use the personal pronouns like "he", "him", or "her" I'm referring to my ex-husband and "his" person. When I use 'you', or 'we', I am talking about 'you' -the reader or the public in general.

THE END...

Day 1

7/11/15

I am completely broken hearted. "He" has left our relationship for another woman. I don't know how to get through this; I cannot stop the tears. Why, oh, why, did "he" do this? My heart and my thoughts will not stop spinning. I cannot rest; oh help me, Lord!

Thank You, Lord; I have no idea of my future! I do not know where to turn. I cannot stop saying, "Why, why did "he" do this?" Thank You, Lord; You understand! I can lay this down at Your feet and see that it is covered by the blood of Your dear Son!

Rule #6 Lay down the *why*. God understands!

"For My thoughts are not your thoughts,

neither are your ways My ways," declares the Lord,

for as the heavens are higher than the earth,

so are My ways higher than your ways,

and My thoughts than your thoughts.

--Isaiah 55:8-9

Day 2

7/25/15

There are just no words…no clear thoughts. No joy, hope, or light! Help me, Lord!

Trust in the Lord with all your heart,
and do not lean on your own understanding.
In all your ways acknowledge Him,
and He will make your paths straight.
Do not be wise in your own eyes;
fear the Lord and turn away from evil.
it will be healing to your body,
and refreshment to your bones.
--Proverbs 3:5-8

Thank You, Lord, for sustaining me, even in this dark place!

Day 3

7/26/15

I would seriously like to believe that my husband really loves me! But the days of believing what "he" says have long gone. There are too many lies stacked up!

And this is so painful. My heart is breaking with each new lie, each pretense. It's so confusing because our relationship has crumbled apart; but there is still love in my heart for "him". What to do with the love?

Thank You, Lord, You understand all of my thoughts. You are able and willing to untangle this part of my life and lead me along Your path. Thank You, Lord, as I hold Your hand; You will show me which way to go. And You will heal my wounds. Thank You, Lord, for being so sweet to me!

The angel of the Lord encamps around those who fear Him,

and He rescues them.

--Psalm 34:7

Day 4

7/28/15

There is no way that I should have peace or that I should have any rest in the midst of this pain! But I do!

Thank You, Lord; You are gracious to me. I know that You are working. You are fully able to calm my heart and encourage me through a dark place. You, Oh Lord, are beautiful and glorious! Thank You for a breath of peace and rest today!

...because of the tender mercy of our God,

with which the Sunrise from on high shall visit us,

to shine upon those who sit in darkness and the shadow of death,

to guide our feet into the way of peace.

--Luke 1:78-79

Day 5

8/31/15

Looking back now--I'm so far from Day 5. I'm writing this on Day 193! Wow!

On Day 5, I wasn't sleeping much--I was so frightened! I had no idea what to do next. I was staying in a friend's vacant house which was almost ready to be on the market! And it was quiet! NO TV, almost no furniture--very quiet. And it was snowing; that made it even quieter! (Even though they sold this place months ago, we still call it the Quiet House.)

The Lord met me there. When I was so confused about what to do, He came to the quiet house, visited with me, comforted me! He showed me His loving care and truth!

Thank You, Lord, for those early days of my journey--You met me there in that sweet, quiet place. Thank You for Day 5; You brought me through!

Because he has loved Me, therefore I will deliver him;

I will set him securely on high, because he has known My name.

He will call upon Me, and I will answer him;

I will be with him in trouble;

I will rescue him, and honor him.

With a long life I will satisfy him,

and let him behold My salvation.

--Psalm 91:14-16

Day 6

9/1/15

It's the most horrible thing to sit with your spouse, to tell the counselors (that you are seeing together) that "he" is with another woman, and to have "him" deny it. This was my Day 6--ick! Then in comes the doubting; is this really happening? Did "he" really? Will this ever end? Ick!

Dear Lord--please keep me. I am so afraid. I'm afraid of the future. I don't know where to go, what to do, or who to be now. Thank You, Lord; You are near!

The cords of death encompassed me,

and the terrors of Sheol came upon me;

I found distress and sorrow.

Then I called upon the name of the Lord:

'O Lord, I beseech Thee; save my life!'

Gracious is the Lord, and righteous;

yes, our God is compassionate.

--Psalm 116:3-5

Day 7

9/17/15

I can imagine that you might feel like I do--that this horrible place you are in is more horrible than anyone has ever endured! And that would be <u>true</u>! It is the most awful pain each of us has ever endured!

But, up against the Love of God...There is a balm; that is the Lord; it can soothe and bring peace! And this Love is just a whisper away!

Take courage, Sisters... Jesus is with you!

Thank You, Lord, for Your nearness! Thank You for Your saving work on the Cross. And Thank You for the soothing of our pain with Yours!

Do not fear, for I have redeemed you;

I have called you by name; you are Mine!

When you pass through the waters,

I will be with you;

and through the rivers, they will not overflow you.

When you walk through the fire, you will not be scorched,

nor will the flame burn you.

--Isaiah 43:1b-2

Day 8

11/7/15

There will be days when it seems like all you can do is slog (barely able to move about, as if you are trying to walk through quick sand with 100 lbs. tied to each leg) around in the self-pity, doubt, worry and frustration! That was my yesterday! And you might just try to correct yourself by condemning yourself. Be warned--both self-pity and condemnation are rooted in lies that raise themselves up against God!

I think the only real solution is to stop, rest, listen and praise the Lord. This will bring Him back into focus! And that's really the only place to find peace!

Thank You, Lord, for yesterday--it brought into full focus--that I must surrender to Your wonderful plan for me each moment. Please readjust my thinking today each time I step off the path into living for self!

> *Listen to me, you who pursue righteousness, who seek the Lord;*
>
> *look to the rock from which you were hewn,*
>
> *and to the quarry, from which you were dug.*
>
> *Indeed the Lord will comfort Zion;*
>
> *He will comfort all her waste places.*
>
> *And her wilderness He will make like Eden,*
>
> *and her desert like the garden of the Lord,*
>
> *joy and gladness will be found in her,*
>
> *thanksgiving and sound of melody.*
>
> *--Isaiah 51:1 and 3*

Day 9

11/10/15

The layers of deception keep unfolding, and it's a fresh, new layer of entrusting myself to God. I cannot ever say this enough--I think the Christian life is full of these new opportunities to trust the Lord. I won't ever 'arrive,' but I have 'arrived' in Christ!

The truth is that no matter what is done to us--no matter the pain, sorrow, anguish from the consequences of the other's behavior…God is unchanged. God is holy, longsuffering, and endless in His love and care for us.

Thank You, Lord; this latest thing has brought me to Your throne again.

Shout for joy, O heavens! And rejoice, O earth!

Break forth into joyful shouting, O mountains!

For the Lord has comforted His people,

and will have compassion on His afflicted.

--Isaiah 49:13

Day 10

11/19/15

It has taken all my strength--and a lot of the Lord's, (Ha Ha)--to step into today. For about two years, I have felt that something was wrong in our marriage--and I've done everything I can to fix it! No one has tried harder.

Thank You, Lord; You have given me the strength to see and to step forward.

Rule #4   God will show you what you need to see. God sees!

Thank You, Lord; You have shown me Your truth.

Rule #3   No one gets to say who I am but God. God says!

And Thank You, Lord; You are taking care of me in Your time.

Rule #5   God's time is perfect. God endures!

I waited patiently for the Lord:

and He inclined to me, and heard my cry.

He brought me up out of the pit of destruction, out of the miry clay;

and He set my feet upon a rock; making my footsteps firm.

--Psalm 40:1-2

Day 11

2/6/16

There is so much confusion in my mind. I don't know what to do! "Cry out to Me, call My name…Jesus."

The name of the Lord is a strong tower:

the righteous runs into it and is safe.

--Proverbs 18:10

Day 12

6/29/15

It was a cold January day…"he" had just stayed somewhere else overnight. My fear is that "he" is leaving me, but "he' says "he's" not. If only this were the end of it or the beginning of the end…but it's not. I'm right in the middle. How long, Lord, is the middle going to last? A week? A month? A year?

Thank You, Lord! I am in Your hands, under Your wings, enveloped in Your Mighty arms. And I wait…to see when this will be over?!

Rule #7   God's arm is long enough to walk with me every step. God loves.

I sought the Lord, and He answered me,

and delivered me from all my fears.

--Psalm 34:4

Day 13

9/24/15

In my journal, about a year ago…

"I cannot make "him" change! I cannot wait until "he" changes…I must run the race You have set before me. I cannot keep waiting for "him" to catch up.

Remind me today, Lord--keep me in the fight.

I think this is so much more about me and my thinking, acting, being, than it is about "him!" I just know, Lord, there will be so many times in my life that I cannot change circumstances or people. So I can keep crashing up against that fact, or I can Thank You, follow You, and let You show me what the fight really is!

Thank You, Lord; the war is always before You. You have clear sight and true knowledge, so You can guide us all the way! Thank You, Lord; You see it all!

For though we walk in the flesh, we do not war according to the flesh,

for the weapons of our warfare are not of the flesh,

but divinely powerful for the destruction of fortresses.

We are destroying speculations

and every lofty thing raised up against the knowledge of God,

and we are taking every thought captive to the obedience of Christ.

--2 Corinthians 10:3-5

Day 14

10/2/15

I feel a little like a derailed train. One day, I'm going in a direction; the next, I am off the tracks completely. Now, my engine is going the other way!

And my prevailing thought is: "I didn't want this!" I never chose for my marriage to end. Or…maybe I did, when I said, "<u>No</u> <u>more</u>!" I can't go on with "him" being with her… and me, and "he's" unwilling to ever tell the truth!

How the Lord must weep over us when we keep walking away from Him! He never says, "That's enough, I give up on you." I'm thankful for that!

Thank You, Lord, You love us forever! You will never leave us. And You desire to walk with us every step of the way!

Rule #7   God's arm is long enough to walk with us every step. God loves!

The mind of a man plans his way,

But the Lord directs his steps.

--Proverbs 16:9

Day 15

And although the actions of this one who used to kiss me are now horrible and cruel, You will never, Lord, never treat me that way, Lord; You love me! And when I am disregarded and even threatened by "him"--Lord, You are always standing near.

Thank You, Lord, when I am walking through what really sounds and feels like death, You are right beside me. Taking care and meeting my needs!

Rule #7 God's arm is long enough to walk with me every step. God loves!

Even though I walk through the valley of the shadow of death,

I fear no evil, for You are with me;

Your rod and Your staff, they comfort me.

--Psalm 23:4

Day 16

10/7/15

Acceptance with Joy…I imagine--I almost always thought I could figure out anything. I could always make a good plan for the next situation! I could order my life to make sense.

But, now I can see that I was wrong! While I could have some measure of success, it was shallow, and there was no real peace in it!

The real peace can be found in God's plan for my life and yours! Seeing that and accepting it is the place to live. And allowing myself to be joyous in His working in my life, I know He has my best and highest in the plan.

Thank You, Lord; I know You have seen my entire life before You. You have joy over me, over my obedience to Your word. You are glorious in Your unconditional love for me. I praise You, Lord; You are beautiful. I accept Your work in my life and praise You for the joy it brings to my heart!

The plans of the heart belong to man,

but the answer of the tongue is from the Lord.

All the ways of a man are clean in his own sight,

but the Lord weighs the motives.

Commit your works to the Lord.

and your plans will be established.

--Proverbs 16:1-3

Day 17

6/29/16

The deepest of all that God has done in me during this time must be:

Rule #3   No one (not even that "guy") gets to say who I am but God. God says!

That is the very foundation of our walk with the Lord.

If I don't stand on what God says, I have nothing but shifting sand! And God has so many things to say about me in relationship to Him! I want to listen and to walk in it. This is the safe place!

Thank You, Lord; You are saying who I am every day of my walk with You. Your child, the love of Your life, Thank You, Lord!

And every one who hears these words of Mine

and does not act upon them,

will be like a foolish man, who built his house upon the sand!

--Matthew 7:26

Day 18

6/29/15

And though I never believed I would be divorced…this is where I am! This is where God is walking with me. Today this is my Christian walk!

I suppose you are here, too…I want to say to you, "God is faithful! He brought me here, to speak to me, to be with me, and He's using this moment to show me Himself! He didn't plan this divorce for me, but is with me…and you. I hope you're finding Him here. He loves you--and longs to walk this journey with you…as well!"

Now to Him who is able to keep you from stumbling,

and to make you stand in the presence of His glory

blameless with great joy

--to the only God our Savior,

through Jesus Christ our Lord,

be glory, majesty, dominion and authority,

before all time and now and forever. Amen.

--Jude 24:25

Day 19

8/31/15

It's true, Lord, I don't always trust You to guide me! I trust myself instead--Ha Ha! I want to figure it all out, plan each step, and weigh each choice. And then I wonder why things aren't working for me!

Thank You, Lord; you know best and most what is for my best good! You are completely able to work out each step of my life. Thank You, Lord!

Behold, I am the Lord, the God of all flesh;

is anything too difficult for Me?

--Jeremiah 32:26

Day 20

10/20/15

Morning Meditation

--Psalm 139:1-6

O Lord, Thou hast searched me and known me! You know everything about me.

Thou dost know when I sit down and when I rise up;

Thou dost understand my thought from afar.

You know what I'm doing and what I'm thinking.

Thou dost scrutinize my path and my lying down,

and art intimately acquainted with all my ways.

You see the directions I'm going, even my sleeping. You know it all. I am known by You!

Even before there is a word on my tongue, Behold,

O Lord, Thou dost know it all.

I can't even think of a word without You knowing it--You know what I'm going to say.

Thou hast enclosed me behind and before, and laid Thy hand upon me.

You have surrounded me with Yourself, protecting me, even though You do know all of me.

> *Such knowledge is too wonderful for me; it is too high,*
>
> *I cannot attain to it.*

You are so amazingly wonderful to love me, even though You know all about me and know my weaknesses and strengths. You know when I walk away from You and You still love me. This is far away from my understanding. I can only accept, by faith Your steadfast love!

Day 21

10/30/15

It's starting to get cold again. It was cold when I left my husband nearly ten months ago. Then I was filled with sadness and confusion!

Today I was joyful when I woke up. I can complete some work. I'm in my own place and I get to spend time with sweet family.

Thank You, Lord; You have given me Your understanding, Your love, Your endurance, courage, perseverance. Thank You, Lord, for each new day.

If you are in a sad, and very difficult place, if you need help, if you need prayer, friends, have physical needs, I hope you'll reach out, tell someone, seek out a local church, charity, or help organization. And most of all, talk to God; He will hear you. He will meet you; He loves you!

Make me know Thy ways, O Lord,

Teach me Thy paths.

Lead me in Thy truth and teach me.

For Thou art the God of my salvation;

for Thee I wait all the day.

--Psalm 25:4-5

Day 22

6/30/15

That first night when I stepped out by faith into God's truth…that might have been the easiest of the hard days. That was the first of many, many days of wrestling with myself!

I'm asking myself, "Who can really accomplish this running of my life--me or the Lord?" Am I going to trust the Lord, or trust myself to run my life? It's a question I get to answer every day of this Christian life.

Thine, O Lord, is the greatness and the power and the glory

and the victory and the majesty;

indeed everything that is in the heavens and the earth;

Thine is the dominion, O Lord, and Thou dost exalt Thyself

as head over all.

--1 Chronicles 29:11

Day 23

7/24/15

Here's the thing about a lie; it's so much more than just a statement. Once it's said, it carries with it some baggage which just multiplies as the days go by. It can influence people and situations and feelings. It may disappear for a while, but will come back with a vengeance, to wreak havoc again. But, really--it has no power!

Here's the thing about the truth; it never changes. It encourages and lifts up; it endures, lives, breathes and trains us. And it carries with it power from God to bring Glory to His name!

Thank You, Lord; You are truth. You do not lie. You will not and have not ever misrepresented Yourself in any way, not even with a tiny white lie! You are light; You are truth. Thank You, Lord!

Rule #2   Don't dialogue with the devil. God is truth!

If you abide in My word, then you are truly disciples of Mine;

and you shall know the truth,

and the truth shall make you free.

--John 8:31-32

Day 24

10/7/15

Lord, Thank You, I am Your child and no can tear me from Your hand. Thank You for sustaining me! I know I belong to You; You are working in and through me. Remind me daily to embrace this!

When pain and sorrow over my broken marriage comes, please meet me and walk with me through it. I can trust You; I know You are trustworthy--You love me! Thank You for loving me!

"Who shall separate us from the love of Christ?

Shall tribulation, or distress, or persecution, or famine,

or nakedness, or peril, or sword?"

Just as it is written,

"For Thy sake we are being put to death all day long;

we are considered as sheep to be slaughtered."

"But in all these things we overwhelmingly conquer

through Him who loved us."

--Romans 8:35-37

Day 25

10/8/15

My life feels a little treacherous. I cannot stop it from the crazy course "he" has set it on!

But I know I am not at "his" mercy. God really is in control of my life. And more and more, I am able to see quickly where I have surrendered to the bondage of taking responsibility for "his" crazy behavior.

Oh, Dear Lord, Thank You for speaking to my heart. Thank You for reminding me in each moment that I belong to You!

Rule #3   No one gets to say who I am but God. God says!

O send out Thy light and Thy truth, let them lead me:

let them bring me to Thy holy hill,

and to Thy dwelling places.

--Psalm 43:3

Day 26

10/31/15

There is a fine line between "Yes, Lord, here it is." And "Oh, I'll deal with that later; I don't want to think about it now!" I can surely package up my problems and put them to the back of my mind to be dealt with by me, in my strength at a later time. But walking in newness of life--that means bringing each thing in my life to the Lord and letting Him work in it. It also means allowing myself to come under His control!

I Thank You, Lord, for as You ask me to do this; You are fully able to work out my life's issues according to Your plan. You are also here--to walk with me, good or bad, happy or sad!

...in reference to your former manner of life, you lay aside the old self,

which is being corrupted in accordance with the lusts of deceit,

and that you be renewed in the spirit of your mind,

and put on the new self,

which in the likeness of God has been created in the righteousness

and holiness of the truth.

--Ephesians 4:22b-24

Day 27

Rule #1   Don't try to figure it out...it could hurt your brain. God knows!

No, try as I might, I cannot figure this out! I never counted on or imagined that this person whom I love, could be so cruel...

Thank You, Lord; You know. You know each pain! In fact, You have endured it and are here with me each step!

He who is steadfast in righteousness will attain to life,

and he who pursues evil will bring about his own death.

--Proverbs 11:19

Day 28

9/15/15

There are so many ups and downs on our life's journey—I tend to measure my success by the ups. And I tend to punish myself for the downs. I'm sure this is not what God intended for His babies! I imagine He doesn't want us to measure or count or compare. This takes our eyes off of Him!

Thank You, Lord; the only measuring up that should be happening is You looking at Your Son Jesus. He died for our sin and imperfection. And now it's our life's work to practice looking through Your eyes instead of ours! And Thank You for empowering us to do so!

For he who boasts, let him boast in the Lord,

for not he who commends himself is approved,

but whom the Lord commends.

--2 Corinthians 10:17-18

Day 29

2/13/16

No matter how many times I go over the journal entries and try to understand what has happened to my life in the last year, it never changes!

Rule #1   Don't try to figure it out…it could hurt your brain. God knows!

The stuff really doesn't change; it happened! But, I have changed. When I look at it now, I am different. I can see more clearly how abusive our relationship was. And I can see the Lord…

The Lord never changed in the entire year. He was with us every moment. The Lord helped me up when I was shaking and crying out in pain. The Lord provided for each day and each fresh start. Thank You, Lord…You are awesome and beautiful and…sweet! I love You, Lord!

> *For I, the Lord, do not change; therefore you,*
>
> *O sons of Jacob, are not consumed.*
>
> *--Malachi 3:6*

Day 30

2/25/16

    I'm a firm believer in not saying bad things about my husband. I know it was partly this that caused me to stay as long as I did and to keep so much from friends and family.

    And there it is…when is honoring actually dishonor, unloving, even damaging? I guess when you sin by trying to cover up someone else's sin--yes, that's wrong!! So when things became so bad that I had to tell the truth about "him" and what "he" was doing, it left me with the devastating notion that it was really--in some way, my fault. Twisted, I know!

    Actually, the truth is something was going on, and it was breaking our marriage! And it was right for me to come into the light and say, "I won't cover it up anymore." Thank You Lord, for the strength and bravery to tell the truth! I Thank You that just because I told the truth it was not my fault.

Pray for us, for we are sure that we have a good conscience,

desiring to conduct ourselves honorably in all things.

--Hebrews 13:18

Day 31

3/2/16

I have had as my aim, my goal, for a long time--probably my entire married life, to get "him" to change. Even though I began to understand that it wasn't my job to change "him," I kept on with it!

And now, in the middle of this, I can see that I still think that I can get "him" to stop. This is not the truth!! Thank You, Lord, for this new insight! Please, O Lord, show me how to live!

Consider and answer me, O Lord, my God;

enlighten my eyes, lest I sleep the sleep of death,

lest my enemy say, 'I have overcome him,'

but I have trusted in Thy lovingkindness;

my heart shall rejoice in Thy salvation.

I will sing to the Lord,

because He has dealt bountifully with me

--Psalm 13:3-6

Day 32

9/15/15

If only there were a formula or a check list, that would tell when your marriage is eroding. Erosion doesn't happen all at once; it takes time! But then, of course, if there were a list--we would all be checking things off each day!

And if there were a list, I would have been more alarmed when "he" started kissing me in random places (i.e. top of my head, on the shoulder) instead of on the lips. And that was almost two years ago. Where was I? What was I thinking! WARNING--GET HELP!

I was getting help; a Godly woman was discipling me! But "he" was already making decisions to sin on purpose to break our marriage!

Thank You, Lord; I can look back now, and see what You were doing in me. I can see and not be afraid. Thank You; there is even joy in all You've done! I can see and be glad!

Rule #4   God will show you what you need to see. God sees!

Behold, as the eyes of servants look to the hand of their master,

as the eyes of a maid to the hand of her mistress;

so our eyes look to the Lord our God,

until He shall be gracious to us.

--Psalm 123:2

Day 33

11/3/15

Having a quick answer is not always the best thing! The world wants us to rush ahead--be aggressive, get things done! But this is not how God wants us to live!

Walking this fine line with the Lord is difficult; I tend to want whatever it is now!! I'm finding that the Lord is making my life into a beautiful piece of music. He is orchestrating a symphony; the timing must be just right for what He is doing in my life!

Thank You, Lord; I can trust You and what You are doing in me! I can lean on You; I can trust You!

Rule #5   God's time is perfect. God endures!

Just as you do not know the path of the wind

and how bones are formed in the womb of a pregnant woman,

so you do not know the activity of God who makes all things.

--Ecclesiastes 11:5

Day 34

3/25/16

> *The eyes of the Lord are toward the righteous,*
> *and His ears are open to their cry.*
> *The face of the Lord is against evildoers,*
> *to cut off the memory of them from the earth.*
> *The righteous cry and the Lord hears*
> *and delivers them out of their troubles.*
> *The Lord is near to the brokenhearted*
> *and saves those who are crushed in spirit.*
> *--Psalm 34:15-18*

Thank You, Lord…

Day 35

6/11/16

I keep having this horrible feeling that I have done something wrong. I keep feeling that filing for divorce was way, way the wrong thing to do. Otherwise, why would "he" be so very mad at me?

The truth is, "he's" mad because I stood up to "him" and "his" lies and because I told the truth. And when 'we' (the 'we' that is each of us) are confronted with the truth against our lies--'we' get mad! No one wants to be wrong because 'we' are absorbed in self! 'We' all want to be right; 'we' want to be okay. And 'we' still think 'we' have some say in our being okay. But 'we' don't.

Rule #3   No one gets to say who I am but God. God Says!

Only God can create a life; only He can change a life. Only He can redeem a life! Thank You Lord for making me Your precious child! Thank You for leading me in Your truth!

For what credit is there if,

when you sin and are harshly treated, you endure it with patience?

But if when you do what is right and suffer for it you patiently endure it,

this finds favor with God.

--1 Peter 2:20

Day 36

5/9/16

Going to the eye doctor should not be so traumatic. But it was… Someone who has known "his" family for a lifetime works there. So when I walk in to have them look at a crack in my glasses, there she is…awkward! Do I just give up and find another eye doc! Good grief!

Thank You, Lord; I survived it. And Thank You, because this and other awkward moments keep me running to You!

Do not trust in a neighbor;

do not have confidence in a friend.

From her who lies in your bosom

guard your lips.

But as for me, I will watch expectantly for the Lord:

I will wait for the God of my salvation.

My God will hear me."

--Micah 7:5 and 7

Day 37

10/4/15

I remember so well what happened a year ago today! We had just finished a big Craft Show, the cars of vendors were everywhere; they blocked us from moving. So—the one I am married to decided to drive up a small hill which was more like a mountain!! And I kept saying, "Please don't do that; you're going to flip our car over." Finally, he stopped and we were able to get out another way.

That was a milestone! I had known for some time that "he" would not listen to me. "He" did not regard me as being of any consequence in our life together. But that day, I really knew "we" were finished! And that was frightening. "His" choice was made!

For a year, I have recalled that day and counted it as a debt "he" owed against me. Today, I want to lay it down! Dear Lord, I want to choose to forgive "him" for trying to hurt me! And to hurt us!

"And forgive us our debts, as we also forgive our debtors."

For if you forgive men for their transgressions,

your heavenly Father will also forgive you."

--Matthew 6:12 and 14

Day 38

11/28/15

Today, I am thankful for a warm and cozy robe; I bought it this week for those chilly days. I know it's a small everyday thing; most people have a robe. But I didn't!

The reason this really is a big thing--I had gotten into the habit of short-changing myself, even on some basic needs, in order to take care of our family. This was really about my thinking that I am inferior all the time. And it is also really about my trying to be lord of my life. Funny thing--how it keeps coming back to that!

Lord, You are Lord!

Rule #3   No one gets to say who you are but God. God says!

But the Father said to his slaves,

Quickly bring out the best robe and put in on him,

and put a ring on his hand and sandals on his feet;

and bring the fattened calf, kill it, and let us eat and be merry:

for this son of mine was dead, and has come to life again,

he was lost and has been found."

And they began to be merry.

--Luke 15:22-24

Day 39

12/23/15

I hadn't counted on this newest revelation… Yesterday, a friend from church had a bypass--and I cried when I spoke to his wife, touched by the fear she might be feeling, and her watch-care over him. When I stopped crying, I realized that the man I gave my life to has stolen our future! Never again do I get to take care of him as I was meant to do! Sad!

Thank You, Lord, You have a plan for my future. You have a way prepared for my heart to care for others. Thank You for taking care of me!

How blessed is the man who has made the Lord his trust,

and hast not turned to the proud, nor to those who lapse into falsehood.

Many, O Lord My God, are the wonders which Thou hast done,

and Thy thoughts towards us;

there is none to compare with Thee;

if I would declare and speak of them,

they would be too numerous to count.

--Psalm 40:4-5

Day 40

1/23/16

We must be willing to lay down the life we have planned for ourselves. We must be willing to let the Lord orchestrate a new fresh life for us, a life full of being used by Him!

I can certainly make plans! Figuring out my entire life--I'm all over that! Thank You, Lord; You are quick to show me when I'm planning away my future and missing what You long to do in my life! Keep me looking to You for Your way…not mine!

Many are the plans in a man's heart,

But the counsel of the Lord, it will stand.

-- Proverbs 19:21

Day 41

3/15/16

I wasn't really prepared to answer my eight year old nephew's questions! "Why aren't you living at your house?" "Where is Uncle-?" "Why are you not with Uncle-?"

Thank You, Lord; You gave me the words to say. And though there was not a way to explain, You led me to say, "You are not old enough to understand but I will explain when you are." Thank You, Lord; You have given me the words over and over during this journey. And the words have been okay. My friends and family have been okay with my words, Your words!

Let the words of my mouth and the meditation of my heart

be acceptable in Thy sight,

O Lord, my rock and my redeemer.

--Psalm 19:14

Day 42

9/6/16

Almost every morning when I open my blinds, I think, "I hope my car is there!" That is because I'm afraid "he" will have taken it away.

I hate that feeling, Lord. The feeling that I have no control over "him," when is "he" going to stop attacking me. When will "he" stop taking things away from me... feeling!

Rule #1 Don't try to figure it out...it could hurt your brain. God knows!

O Dear Lord, please help me! I don't want to live in fear every day! Please give me peace in this. I know "he's" attacking me because I stood up to "him" and the lies. O Help me, Lord! Keep me safe!

And the Lord said to Paul in the night by a vision,
"Do not be afraid any longer, but go on speaking and do not be silent;
for I am with you, and no man will attack you,
for I have many people in this city."
--Acts 18:9-10

Day 43

2/1/16

Some days, like today, there are no words! There are questions; there is the WOW but no words come!

But Dear Lord, You are the same God as yesterday and last year! You love me the same; You are unchangeable! You see everything, know everything, and nothing is a surprise to You. Thank You; no matter what circumstance comes my way, You are always there, loving me!

And there is no creature hidden from His sight,

But all things are open and laid bare to the eyes of Him

with whom we have to do.

--Hebrews 4:13

Day 44

2/4/16

It is a difficult thing--navigating a sorrowful place in your life--without the self-pity that comes to us! And people aren't certain what to do with you! And you don't even know what to do with yourself! And as you walk with the Lord, you don't really want everyone to focus on the sorrowful things, but rather on the real joy of the Lord in you! So this is the purpose of my life? To show the faithfulness of God Himself!

Dear Lord, please help me to lay aside the searching for meaning and figuring things out. Please help me trust You--to really entrust my life to You! My life will contain just the right amount of sorrow and just the right amount of joy. Thanks to You, I will trust in You!

Many are saying, "Who will show us any good?"

Lift up the light of Thy countenance upon us, O Lord!

"You have put gladness in my heart,

more than when their grain and new wine abound.

In peace will I both lie down and sleep,

for You alone, O Lord, make me to dwell in safety."

--Psalm 4:6-8

Day 45

Even though I know my life may not be perfect, I still want it to be, every moment of every day, etc. And it's the search for perfection that takes my eyes from the Lord and causes me to look at me.

Warning…this will lead to folly!

Only when I am looking at Him and being with Him, do I know 'perfection,' not a thing, but a person… The Person of Christ! Thank You Lord, that You gave Your perfect Son to make me whole!

And we have come to know and have believed the love

which God has for us.

God is love, and the one who abides in love abides in God,

and God abides in him.

By this, love is perfected with us,

so that we may have confidence in the day of judgment;

because as He is, so also are we in this world.

--1 John 4:16-17

Day 46

9/5/15

I thought marriage would be rosy and sweet, with a little excitement, some adventure, and then, later, a bit of pain, intermingled with lots of joy! I was wrong!! But I tried as hard as I could to make it look like what I thought it was supposed to be; maybe that's the problem.

Here's what I know now. I don't know what marriage is supposed to look like! And now it has failed and I'm looking around saying…what hope is there???

Thank You, Lord; my only hope is You. You define each of our lives, tirelessly loving us each moment. You're working out for our highest and best good, all the turmoil of our lives. And You're working all of it to Your glory!

"Though He slay me, I will hope in Him.

Nevertheless I will argue my ways before Him.

This also will be my salvation,

for a godless man may not come before His presence."

--Job 13:15-16

Day 47

10/9/15

Today, I am thankful for two white tubs. They were among the things I got from my house. And they are the perfect size for dishes. Wash and rinse, wash and rinse. When you bake for a living, washing dishes is a big thing! And I'm finally in a sort of groove with it at my new place, where I'm the only dishwasher.

It's a small thing, I know! But Thank You, Lord for two white dish tubs. Thank You for caring about the small things; this shows me that You care for me in the small and the big!

As a shepherd cares for his herd in the day

when he is among his scattered sheep,

so I will care for My sheep

and deliver them from all the places to which they were scattered

on a cloudy and gloomy day.

--Ezekiel 34:12

Day 48

11/26/15

Oh Lord, remind me to meet You in the morning of a new day! These days, if I don't meet with You, I really miss it! I want to stay close by; You help me walk through this mystery that is Your life in me!

Thank You, Lord, for meeting me in the morning and each moment from dawn to sleep! Thank You for ordering my day, showing me Your plans, and helping to fix my eyes on You!

In the morning, O Lord, Thou wilt hear my voice;

In the morning I will order my prayer to Thee

and eagerly watch.

--Psalm 5:3

Day 49

11/23/15

I hadn't counted on some people's reactions…sometimes they just walk away when I mention what's really going on in my life regarding "him."

So many friends have comforted me; I know they are praying and sharing in my pain. But a few have no grace for hearing about things. It's just a reminder to me that You, Lord, will never walk away. You have a forbearing spirit. You understand the un-understandable. You walk each step with us. And You do not ever tire of us! Maybe that is what longsuffering means?

A friend loves at all times,

And a brother is born for adversity.

--Proverbs 17:17

Day 50

12/10/15

Today, I am thankful for my laundry helpers! I can't do a thing about dirty laundry with my broken arm! They come by my house, pick up a load, and in a day or so, it comes back clean, folded, and beautiful!

This makes me think of You, Lord. You generously loved us and washed us with the amazing sacrifice of Your Son. And You have enfolded us into this beautiful, moment by moment walk with You! Thank You, Lord!

And such were some of you,

but you were washed, but you were sanctified,

but you were justified in the name of the Lord Jesus Christ,

and in the Spirit of our God.

--1 Corinthians 6:11

Day 51

2/5/16

I am broken hearted--to imagine that you might be in the middle of this, like me! Please take courage, God is here with us! When the mountain in front of you seems way too big, God is here. When the pain is too much, God is here. God will never leave us or forsake us!

Thank You, Lord; You love Your children. Thank You for taking care of us!

"Have I not commanded you?

Be strong and courageous!

Do not tremble or be dismayed,

for the Lord you God is with you wherever you go."

--Joshua 1:9

Day 52

3/31/16

Waiting for the Lord to order my day is good practice! It's wonderful to walk in the truth that He knows me, knows what's best for me. And He will show me! So I stop and say, Thank You, Lord; You know the best direction for me to go today. And You will take care of my path!

Today there is a lot of work to do; I am getting ready for baking things that will be picked up on Saturday. Happy things--a 1st Birthday, a 70th Birthday and a Baby on the way! Thank You, Lord; today You're helping me help others celebrate with sweets!

> *"Let your light shine before me in such a way*
>
> *that they might see your good works,*
>
> *and glorify your Father who is in heaven."*
>
> --Matthew 5:16

Day 53

8/1/16

About the time I left my husband, there was a new song on the radio; it is called "Broken Together." I've heard that song many times in the last year and a half.

It seems that was the problem all along: "he" could not, would not be broken. And to this day, "he" is still raising "himself" up against God and His truth. "He" does not understand that in brokenness there is redemption. Walking in pride and self, "he" actually has it all backwards!

Thank You, Lord; You have shown me during this time that brokenness leads to salvation, peace and joy. Thank You, Lord, though I still shrink back from brokenness, I know You will always meet me there and walk with me through it.

O Lord, open my lips,

that my mouth may declare Thy praise.

For though dost not delight in sacrifice,

otherwise I would give it;

thou art not pleased with burnt offering.

The sacrifices of God are a broken spirit;

a broken and a contrite heart,

O God, Thou wilt not despise.

--Psalm 51:15-17

Day 54

2/5/16

Even though it's firmly planted in my mind…I keep coming back to it!

Rule #6 Lay down the *why*. God understands!

Loving your spouse can be a beautiful thing that can be easy and difficult. Why did "he" keep choosing to walk away!! I'm facing the fact that this will never make sense to me. It will never seem right!

Thank You, Lord; this is something over which I have no control. It's something that I get to surrender to You moment by moment. Help me see the joy in laying this continually at Your feet!

It is He who made the earth by His power,

who established the world by His wisdom;

and by His understanding He has stretched out the heavens.

--Jeremiah 10:12

Day 55

6/29/15

At the first of this journey, You gave me Rule #2 Don't believe anything "he" says. Because I was being emotionally tossed about by "his" lies, it seemed to help. Then, after a while, You began to transform Rule #2.

I was beginning to argue back and forth with the lies! "He" would say this or that…is it true? One day my sweet counselor said, "Don't Dialogue with the devil." And it stuck with me! What she meant was that I, (we) don't need to talk back and forth with that liar. Instead, as soon as a thought comes to my head, I can apply the truth of God and who He is to the thought.

Thank You, Lord; when the thoughts come, I can go straight to "Thank You, Lord; I am Your precious child, created by You and deeply loved by You." Thank You Lord; You tell the truth!

Rule #2 Don't Dialogue with the devil. God is Truth!

O God, do not remain quiet;

do not be silent, and O God, do not be still.

For, behold, Thine enemies make an uproar;

and those who hate Thee have exalted themselves.

They make shrewd plans against Thy people.

And conspire together against Thy treasured ones.

…let them be ashamed and dismayed forever;

and let them be humiliated and perish,

that they may know that Thou alone, whose name is the Lord,

art the Most High over all the earth.

--Psalm 83:1-3, 17-18

Day 56

8/3/16

"He" cannot win in the middle of "his" sin, "his" tormenting spirit, "his" manipulation… I am truly untouched! Because I belong to the Lord and I'm walking with the Lord, "he" cannot win in any action "he" takes to hurt and destroy me. What "he" has clung to with all "his" might, will be "his" undoing!

Often I'm reminded of the night I left. The next day when I returned to the house, "he" had packed and hidden some cherished decorative dishes from me. "His" wife left so he took some dishes. This has always puzzled me! But I think it shows where "his" treasure is…certainly I'm not "his" treasure nor was our marriage.

Thank You, Lord, for showing me truth. I am Your most prized possession! And You are the most important thing in my life. Please always show me if I start to choose something over You!

The way of a fool is right in his own eyes,
But a wise man is he who listens to counsel.

--Proverbs 12:15

Day 57

12/10/15

I have had such difficulty reconciling "his" behavior with "his" profession of faith! I had assumed that not only our marriage commitment, and also our commitment to walk with the Lord were set in stone, so to speak. But it appears that the rejection was not only "his" commitment to our marriage, but also "his" walk with the Lord.

As a result, beyond the sadness over the state of our marriage, there is a real sadness that I feel, especially when I think of "him" having lost "his" way with the Lord. If only "he" could realize that the light of the Lord really is surrounding us and true repentance is always a millisecond away.

If we say we have fellowship with Him

and yet walk in the darkness,

we lie and do not practice the truth;

But if we walk as He Himself is in the Light,

we have fellowship with one another,

and the blood of Jesus His Son cleanses us from all sin.

--1 John 1:6-7

Day 58

8/9/16

Most nights I talk to the Lord about what I did that day. And when we go over it, I can say, "I got some things accomplished. Good job!"

But some days I wonder if my life is making a difference for the Lord? Lord please show me each day, what my work is to be. I want to serve You, Lord.

If anyone serves Me, let him follow Me;

and where I am,

there shall My servant also be;

if anyone serves Me, the Father will honor him.

--John 12:26

Day 59

8/25/16

Oh Lord, please be with me; I'm on a bit of a roller coaster. Once again there are just no words for the craziness around me!

Bring me back, Lord, to looking at You. That's the only way to survive this craziness that's been coming at me! I am resting in You; You're the same God who has been here this entire year, all these years!

> *But as for me, I am like a green olive tree in the house of God;*
>
> *I trust in the lovingkindness of God forever and ever,*
>
> *I will give Thee thanks forever, because Thou hast done it.*
>
> *And I will wait on Thy name, for it is good,*
>
> *in the presence of Thy godly ones.*
>
> --Psalm 52:8-9

Day 60

8/25/16

A Meditation —-Psalm 46

God is our refuge and strength,

a very present help in trouble.

Therefore we will not fear, though the earth should change,

and though the mountains slip into the heart of the sea;

though the waters roar and foam,

though the mountains quake at its swelling pride.

There is a river whose streams make glad the city of God.

The holy dwelling places of the Most High.

God is in the midst of her, she will not be moved;

God will help her when morning dawns.

The nations made an uproar, the kingdoms tottered;

He raised His voice, the earth melted.

The Lord of hosts is with us;

the God of Jacob is our stronghold.

Come, behold the works of the Lord,

Who has wrought desolations in the earth.

He makes wars to cease to the end of the earth;

He breaks the bow and cuts the spear in tow;

He burns the chariots with fire.

'Cease striving and know that I am God;

I will be exalted among the nations, I will be exalted in the earth.'

The lord of hosts is with us;

The God of Jacob is our stronghold.

Day 61

10/15/15

I asked the why question today; there is still no answer, and it's been 231 days since I left. I'm still not free of it. The house is still sitting there; it's a wreck from "him" fixing it. Even though a realtor listed it, it's not being shown. I can't get in for my things.

I guess I must trust You again. I must look into Your beautiful eyes. Oh my Dear Lord, where would I be without You? Thank You, Lord; it will be enough today to not know why! It is enough to know You and all Your awesome ways.

Rule #6   Lay down the Why. God understands!

Do not be as the horse or as the mule which have no understanding,

Whose trappings include bit and bridle to hold them in check,

otherwise they will not come near to you.

Many are the sorrows of the wicked,

but he who trusts in the Lord, lovingkindness shall surround him.

--Psalm 32:9-10

Day 62

10/17/15

> *For where your treasure is, there will your heart be also.*
>
> *--Luke 12:34*

It has taken some time but I can see now that my treasure was my marriage. In a way, it became my ultimate goal. If only I will meet someone. If only he will love me. If only we will live happily ever after!

Thank You, Lord, for showing me this idol in my life. Remind me that I am to be ready to serve You. Remind me that everything You bring into my life is for Your glory, not mine.

> *Blessed are those slaves whom the master shall find*
>
> *on the alert when he comes;*
>
> *truly I say to you,*
>
> *that he will gird himself to serve,*
>
> *and have them recline at the table,*
>
> *and will come up and wait on them.*
>
> *--Luke 12:37*

Day 63

1/5/16

With the New Year comes the expectation that there is a fresh start. That by our sheer will, we can turn the corner and leave behind whatever was! Instead, I think it's a continuation of following the Lord.

Pay attention to this truth so you don't get tangled up in expectations full of fluffy kittens and rosy days. It is a lie of satan, and it's tied up in our longing for perfection; whatever that is!

Oh Lord, help me see Your perfection so I can recognize Your great gifts, even when they come looking like a broken wing. I would rather have brokenness than a moment without the safety of Your wings covering me!

He will cover you with His pinions,

and under His wings you may seek refuge;

His faithfulness is a shield and bulwark.

--Psalm 91:4

Day 64

8/18/16

One thing I have noticed about my new life…it's a little easier to give grace to people.

I imagine it's the result of suffering and things taking on new meaning when you've been through hideous, destructive pain and back!! It gets easier to let go of what used to be a little annoying bit of the world. When you know God is indeed big enough, and you realize that the little things don't take anything away from you, for you are safe in His blessed arms.

There is no need to diminish others or be upset when you are relying on Him for your needs, your very worth! God is big and He loves us; He wants to be in relationship with us. We are His; we are His!

Therefore having been justified by faith,

we have peace with God through our Lord Jesus Christ,

through whom also we have obtained our introduction by faith

into this grace in which we stand;

and we exult in hope of the glory of God.

--Romans 5:1- 2

Day 65

No matter how I try to make my brain believe this has happened in my life, my brain just cannot believe it. I must trust the Lord for the truth; I must wait for Him to show me and then trust Him to tell the truth. Very, very hard!!

Thank You, Lord, I can wait on You. You will direct me and my thoughts in Your time.

Rule #5   God's time is perfect. God endures!

You will give me a sense of peace in the midst of this life of Yours, my life in Christ! You will endure with me and lead me. It will be okay!

Blessed is the man who trusts in the Lord

and whose trust is the Lord.

For he will be like a tree planted by the water,

that extends its roots by a stream

and will not fear when the heat comes;

but its leaves will be green,

and it will not be anxious in a year of drought

nor cease to yield fruit.

--Jeremiah 17:7-8

Day 66

7/27/16

Have you ever noticed that when you're sipping your snow cone with a straw, pretty soon nothing is coming out. If you look into the straw, there is nothing. But if you look at the whole cup, there's lots of snow cone left! A change in perspective makes all the difference!

When we are looking directly at our life situations, problems…that's all we're going to see. But stepping back can give us a bit of a new, better perspective!

Thank You Lord; You see everything about our lives. And You will show us in Your time what we need to see.

Rule #3   God will show you what you need to see. God sees!

Come, you children, listen to me;
I will teach you the fear of the Lord.
Who is the man who desires life,
and loves length of days that he may see good?
--Psalm 34:11-12

Day 67

2/6/16

Do I define my whole life by the bad stuff? Oh Lord, I hope not! What to be thankful for today?? Thankful for breath, a place to be and provisions from You, Lord! You are wonderful, Oh Lord!

For I will not trust in my bow,

nor will my sword save me.

But Thou has saved us from our adversaries,

and Thou hast put to shame those who hate us.

In God we have boasted all day long,

and we will give thanks to Thy name forever.

--Psalm 44:6-8

Day 68

6/18/16

    I have spent most of my life trying to avoid pain. When I was a girl, I was avoiding rejection by friends and family. As an adult--it's the really the same.

    And while it's true that we have the possibility of being rejected our whole lives, what we do with that is entirely up to us. When I was a child, I would wear it, but now I can make a choice to bring it to You, Lord!

    Thank You, Lord; You are using the real pain of this world to bring me closer to dependence on You. You really are big enough for my whole life!

> *Blessed is the man who perseveres under trial;*
>
> *for once he has been approved,*
>
> *he will receive the crown of life,*
>
> *which the Lord has promised to those who love Him.*
>
> *--James 1:12*

Day 69

9/6/16

For months and months, I have gotten a sense of the craziness "he" is living in, I keep hearing things…

And although it's been rough going, I have been doing okay. If not for the Lord walking with me each step, I might be living the crazy too. He has shown me peace and endurance, especially in the super tough times.

Thank You, Lord; You are teaching me to walk with You! And it makes a difference! And You are letting me see the despair I would be experiencing, if not for following You. I can never turn back from following, no matter what!

No harm befalls the righteous,

but the wicked are filled with trouble.

--Proverbs 12:21

Day 70

6/1/16

How can it be that even after all You have shown me in the last three years, I still think I am smart enough to run my own life, HA! Oh Lord, may I always see You in the midst of the confusion that I have gotten myself into!

Please, Lord, as I praise You--let me see Your face! Thank You, Lord!

The Lord bless you and keep you;

the Lord make His face shine upon you; and be gracious to you;

the Lord lift up His countenance on you,

and give you peace.

--Numbers 6:24-26

Day 71

10/1/15

There are so many stories of how people are giving and helping me! This week a huge tip came from a sweet couple; it seems so over the top.

After being in the desert for a couple of years, it's a surprise. Don't get me wrong, God was there with me in the desert! But it was hard! Now, I feel like the abundance has come, and I want to figure out how to keep it coming! Ha Ha!

Thank You, Lord; You walk with us every day!

Rule #7 God's arm is long enough to walk with me every step. God loves!

Thank You, Lord; Your love is everlasting. And Your abundance is so perfect that it takes on many faces. Thank You, Lord; You know me and how Your abundance should look in my life today!

For Thou art my hope:

O Lord God, Thou art my confidence from my youth.

By Thee I have been sustained from my birth;

Thou art He who took me from my mother's womb;

my praise is continually of Thee.

--Psalm 71:5-6

Day 72

2/21/16

Yesterday was the one year anniversary of my leaving home. I thought it might be a tough day so I tried to gear up my heart for it by thinking positive, being thankful, and by doing laundry!

So, I'm at the laundromat folding laundry, and I pick up a pillowcase. I need lots of pillows to get into the perfect sleep position: between the knees, behind my back, etc. And that means I have a lot of pillowcases.

Now, every time I pick up a pillowcase, I think, "This one matches the sheets that are locked in my house. And I think "he's" gonna be mad because I took the pillowcases and there aren't any to match "his" sheets."

Thank You, Lord, for the time to do laundry and for soft and cozy pillowcases. Thank You for knowing just what we need. Thank You for providing for me, for a year, and forever! And Thank You; You do not seek Your own, but our highest and best good!

In God, I have put my trust,

I shall not be afraid.

What can man do me?

--Psalm 56:10

Day 73

8/27/16

It should not be my aim to imagine or try to place myself into the will of God…to present my meager self to Him in order to create my own newness of life. I know I do have the choice to surrender to Him, but what He creates out of my surrendered life--well, that is the beautiful mystery that is the Christian journey! Thank You, Lord, for Your beautiful plan for me!

...and He died for all, that they who live

shall no longer live for themselves,

but for Him who died and rose again on their behalf.

"Therefore if any man is in Christ, he is a new creature;

the old things passed away;

behold, new things have come."

--2 Corinthians 5:15 and 17

Day 74

4/25/16

> *Though I walk in the midst of trouble, Thou wilt revive me;*
> *Thou wilt stretch forth Thy hand against the wrath of my enemies.*
> *And Thy right hand will save me.*
>
> *--Psalm 138:7*

Since I left behind so many of my possessions and they have been locked in our house, it has been frustrating. "He" would sometimes throw my things away. Here's a bit of the struggle…

To Go Through the Trash, Or Not?? That is the Question!

I will look like a fool, a dumpster diving fool!

Rule #3 Only God gets to say who I am. God says!

By digging through the trash, I become, well, trash? "He's" saying, You are worthless!

I am not trash! I am God's treasure! Rule #3

What can "he" take away from me, really! Am I not having faith in God?

I might get something back that I can use and enjoy! God can/does supply all my needs! I trust the Lord.

Rule #4 God will show you what you need to see. God sees!

Why should I do this? Am I just trying to get back something "he" stole from me?

Am I giving in to more of "his" manipulation? I will never understand this. I feel so angry!

Rule #1 Don't try to figure it out…it could hurt your brain. God knows!

I want to prove that "he" is doing something wrong. I want power over "him," to take away "his" power over me!!

It is not my job to prove that "he" is walking in sin. This is not a fight of flesh and blood, but a spiritual battle!

Rule #8 God, indeed, has more power than everyone and everything. God is!

And, yes, I did go through the trash that day. I got some Christmas lights, garland, a tablecloth, a Tupperware measuring cup and a ceramic pot that my sister had given me. Every piece was a treasure! Thank You, Lord!!

Day 75

8/15/16

I spent tonight reading through my journal from last year. There were several notes from "him" mentioned. These notes would say, "I love you, I'm so sorry, will you forgive me." Of course they were usually delivered when "his" car was at her house. So I had to realize that "he" was not being truthful, but manipulative.

There was a long time of confusion in this journey! You see, I wanted to forgive and I was waiting for our marriage to work out. Even now, I get the little thoughts, darty (thoughts sent like darts to my soul) 'what if,' 'what if I could just go back.' (remember, the 'what if' thoughts are a tool in the hands of Satan. God never says 'what if.' He says 'I am!')

So, when I put "his" "I love you, come back," spoken when "he" is walking in adultery, up against God's "I am, I love you, you are Mine" spoken in love...there is no turning back. Only stepping out, day by day, to walk with my Lord.

The secret of the Lord is for those who fear Him,

and He will make them know His covenant.

My eyes are continually toward the Lord,

for He will pluck my feet out of the net.

--Psalm 25:14-15

Day 76

9/14/16

The revelation…"he" has never had a truly contrite heart!

I have been waiting all this time; but I wasn't fully sure why I was waiting. Now I know; I've been waiting for the contrition. For "him" to finally admit to "his" part, in a real, true way. "I have done….," "I understand what this has done…," I am truly so sorry for having done…." "How can I repair what I have done?"

These statements could have opened up a dialogue between us. And the continuation of this kind of statements and this attitude might have produced some civility in our relationship.

I Thank You, Lord; these words have not been spoken and acted upon. And Thank You, Lord; You have sustained me without them. I can trust You in my life without "him." And I can let go of the longing for those words. Keep me safe in Your loving arms. I love You, Lord!

Thus says the Lord,

"Heaven is My throne, and the earth is My footstool.

Where then is a house you could build for Me?

And where is a place that I may rest?

For My hand made all these things;

thus all these things came into being." declares the Lord.

But to this one I will look to him who is humble and contrite of spirit,

and who trembles at My word.

--Isaiah 66:1-2

Day 77

12/12/15

When we are traveling through the trials--the big ones--it is, in a way, easier to cling to Him! But when our world settles down, and we can breathe and not want to scream and cry and ask "why," it's a bit harder to walk in His presence. We don't feel that we need Him as much to survive.

I think this is really the time to see Him proven in the small everyday stuff. It is the time to have His deep love for us growing down deep in us, and for us to be rooted and grounded in Him! It is good to rest in Him, gathering the truth about us, being ever ready for God's next adventure!

Thank You, Lord, for this lovely day to be with You. Thank You that I may dwell in Your sweetness and light and rest in You.

Rest in the Lord and wait patiently for Him.

--Psalm 37:7a

And let endurance have its perfect result,

that you may be perfect and complete,

lacking in nothing.

--James 1:4

Day 78

6/18/16

When it's all said and done, my goal is to walk with You, Lord. I can do none other! Please keep me following You and guard my heart from evil schemes!!

Be of sober spirit, be on the alert.
Your adversary, the devil, prowls about like a roaring lion,
seeking someone to devour.
But resist him, firm in your faith,
knowing that the same experiences of suffering are being accomplished
by your brethren who are in the world.
--1 Peter 5:8-9

Day 79

8/29/16

 How many times will I skip ahead, thinking You have left me? Curse these highways of lies about who You are…They have ruled my life!

 You love me. You are the same Father as yesterday, last week, month, last year, 557 days ago… I know You hear me; I know You see me!! Thank You, Lord, as my dear sister reminded me today… You will not leave me! You are for me!

I have called upon Thee, for Thou wilt answer me, O God;

incline Thine ear to me, hear my speech.

Wondrously show Thy lovingkindness,

O Savior of those who take refuge at

Thy right hand from those who rise up against them.

Keep me as the apple of the eye;

hide me in the shadow of Thy wings.

--Psalm 17:6-8

Day 80

9/15/16

In the course of a day, we face so many situations where others will "pronounce" on our lives. To me, this is when friend or foe says. "Your problem is," "You can't," "If only," "That will be hard; you better give up." These pronouncements are a great opportunity for:

Rule #3   No one gets to say who I am but God. God says!

If only I can meet these things with the truth of who God says I am--WOW!

Thank You, Lord; You have a pronouncement of Your own. You say that You have made me perfectly! You can--I can--do all things through Christ! There are no "If onlys" with You. You know the plans You have for me! And "hard," Lord, You break "hard" to bits with Your joy and peace.

Thus says your Lord, the Lord, even your God

who contends with His people,

"Behold, I have taken out of your hand the cup of reeling;

the chalice of My anger, you will never drink it again.

And I will put it into the hand of your tormentors, who have said to you,"

'Lie down that we may walk over you!

You have even made your back like the ground,

and like a street for those who walk over it.'

--Isaiah 51:22-23

Day 81

10/9/16

It is hard for me to imagine that there is another wife in the world who is more surprised than I to find herself in this place. I wake up every day and say, "My life is gone, what do I do now?"!

Oh Lord, please write a new message on my life!! I need the fresh joy every morning!

Then your light will break out like the dawn,

and your recovery will speedily spring forth;

and your righteousness will go before you;

the glory of the Lord will be your rear guard.

Then you will take delight in the Lord,

and I will make you ride on the heights of the earth;

and I will feed you with the heritage of Jacob your father,

for the mouth of the Lord has spoken.

--Isaiah 58:8 and 14

Day 82

And NO, I'm not dreaming all of this--although I wish it were a dream. Then I could just wake up and POOF--all would be well!

Thank You, Lord; You are very near to the broken hearted. You hear and see and live in me. Please keep me in truth, not in dreams!

In thee, O Lord, I have taken refuge;

let me never be ashamed.

In Thy righteousness deliver me, and rescue me:

incline Thine ear to me, and save me.

--Psalm 71:1-2

Day 83

10/15/15

It has been a tough weekend: our Ladies Retreat. I usually have a great time; but this year…It's almost as if I won't let myself be happy!

It is one of the super hard things about this new life that the Lord is forming in me: I am having to lay down a lot of self and let myself take up whatever the Lord is doing! It's an act of worship to give myself over to His plans.

Thank You, Lord; I praise You! You are glorious; You are beautiful. Thank You for letting me walk in new life!

Blessed is the man who listens to me,

watching daily at my gates,

waiting at my doorposts.

For he who finds me finds life,

and obtains favor from the Lord.

--Proverbs 8:34-35

Day 84

9/8/16

When you are on your own, some things are hard to do. I have struggled again and again with the giant trash cans. They are just too big and unsteady for me to wheel out to the curb every week!

So let me paint you a picture: Here I am pushing the super full, big blue to the street yesterday. You must keep in mind--I still have the little gimpy, formerly broken arm, and the currently getting stronger brand new knee. I get to the curb and the wheels go out from under the trash can and SPLAT! I'm in the street with a giant bump on my forehead, a bruise coming up on my cheek, various other bruises and scrapes, and people are driving by...HELLO!

Thank You, Lord; sometimes we fall down. But You are always with us. Thank You that I hit my head on the hard plastic can, instead of the pavement! I didn't injure any of my "new" parts. Please send me a solution because bleeding in the street is no good! Thank You, Lord, for keeping us; we're Your children!

For I hope in Thee, O Lord.

Thou wilt answer, O Lord my God.

For I said, "May they not rejoice over me,

who, when my foot slips, would magnify themselves against me."

--Psalm 38:15-16

Day 85

7/3/15

There are times when self-pity creeps in… At first it can be subtle, but in the end, it's just horribly destructive. It's because self-pity is all about me and not at all about the Lord! And any time I'm there…I'm looking the wrong way.

I've spent plenty of time asking: 'why did "he" do that?' And finally, I saw what it was doing to me…directing me away for my Lord. And while I have no doubt that God understands my question, I also know He always wants to be the answer. "Because I love you, dear child" and "Because I am working to bring you to look more and more like Me." Thank You, Lord; You hold my life in Your hand, and I can rest there!

Rule #6   Lay down the *why*. God understands!

"For I know the plans I have for you," declares the Lord,

"plans for welfare and not for calamity, to give you a future and a hope.

Then you will call upon Me and come and pray to Me

and I will listen to you!"

--Jeremiah 29:11-12

Day 86

2/13/16

Valentine's Day is tomorrow. Of course I've been remembering last year.

I received a lovely card, which was in a really big envelope. I later found out that "he" bought two cards and flowers! When I told "him" that "her" card was not going to fit in the envelope, because "he" had put my card in "her" envelope--"he" didn't really appreciate the humor of it! Ha Ha!, I had to laugh; it was so absurd!

Thank You, Lord; my love card from You always fits. It is fully lovely, perfect for me! Your love is true and forever, never failing. I can believe it when You show me Your Love, Your Glorious Self, and Your Jesus, who died for me. Thank You, Lord, for the most precious Valentine of all!

I Love Thee, O Lord, my strength.

The Lord is my rock and my fortress and my deliverer,

my God, my rock, in whom I take refuge;

my shield and the horn of my salvation, my stronghold.

I call upon the Lord, who is worthy to be praised,

and I am saved from my enemies.

Psalm 18:1-3

Day 87

4/25/16

    This entire way, I have practiced walking closely with the Lord. But of course, tough decisions still crop up from time to time! And sometimes, I just don't know what to do.

    Thank You, Lord. You are with me; You will direct my path. You will counsel me! Lord, please keep me walking in Your way! Keep me from the ways of the wicked!

> *Many are the sorrows of the wicked:*
> *but he who trusts in the Lord,*
> *lovingkindness shall surround him.*
> *Be glad in the Lord and rejoice you righteous ones,*
> *and shout for joy all you who are upright in heart!*
>   --Psalm 32:10-11

Day 88

9/25/16

My heart is heavy for a young woman I know. She is angry, bearing a grudge. I have tried to talk with her, but she has decided to continue in this.

Thank You, Lord; keep reminding me to lay down myself and my way. Remind me that You are for me, no matter who or what is against me. Thank You, Lord; You are forgiveness. You are redemption. You are peace and grace and love! As I walk with You, You will be all of these things to me, for me, and through me. I can lay down my selfishness and pride and take up Your cross! And with each little darty thought, I can turn to You, lay it aside, and follow You!

> *As for you, my son Solomon,*
>
> *know the God of your father,*
>
> *and serve Him with a whole heart and a willing mind;*
>
> *for the Lord searches all hearts,*
>
> *and understands every intent of the thoughts.*
>
> *If you seek Him, He will let you find Him;*
>
> *but if you forsake Him, He will reject you forever.*
>
> *--1 Chronicles 28:9*

Day 89

7/18/16

It's so frustrating when we're in a situation that we can't change; Ha Ha, which is most of life!!

When we are in the right, we know it, everyone around us knows it…but still nothing, we can't force the other to make it right!! So we have two choices: keep walking with the Lord, or try with all our might to get the situation to turn out 'right!' This is the war in me now.

Thank You, Lord. You will show me the way even when I'm not certain I can see it, You will show me! And You will make right the wrong in Your way, Your time, Your might!

Rule #8   God, indeed, has more power than everyone and everything. God is!

Therefore the wicked will not stand in the judgment,

nor sinners in the assembly of the righteous.

For the Lord knows the way of the righteous,

but the way of the wicked will perish.

--Psalm 1:6

Day 90

4/21/16

I may have been looking at this all wrong…having as my goal to get 'my share' of the house and things. I may have been missing the point.

Maybe this has never been and will never be about fairness, but it may be about following the Lord--rain or shine. Winning might be losing; losing might be winning.

Oh Lord, please help me step out of the swimming, teaming crazy pool--this situation with trying to get my share. And help me Lord; to step into Your strong, welcoming arms. Wrap me in the safety of Your presence.

Thank You that I am not to be enslaved by fear or "his" bullying' I am Yours; Thank You, Lord!

For you have not received a spirit of slavery leading to fear again,

but you have received a spirit of adoption as sons

by which we cry out, 'Abba Father.'

--Romans 8:15

Day 91

2/14/16

A Meditation of Joy

Awake, awake, put on strength.

O arm of the Lord;

awake as in the day of old, the generation of long ago.

Was it not Thou who cut Rahab to pieces?

Who pierced the dragon?

Was it not Thou who dried up the sea,

the waters of the great deep;

Who made the depths of the sea a pathway

for the redeemed to cross over.

So the ransomed of the Lord will return,

and come with joyful shouting to Zion;

and everlasting joy will be on their heads.

They will obtain gladness and joy.

And sorrow and sighing will flee away.

--Isaiah 51:9-11

Day 92

7/20/15

Right now when you're in the middle of this process, someone may want you to act, or be a certain way. You may even be wanting to be so far in the process. Or you may perceive that from me, or from God! As if you're hearing: 'Act right or else!!'

Please, sweet sister, rest! It is ok to just be with the Lord. He loves you. He has a plan for you, but I think not in the way we imagine. I think His plan for us is to rest in Him, be with Him, and listen for Him!

I know He will show us the way. He is standing by our side. He is surrounding us, mighty to protect us and enough for your every moment. Thank You, Lord, for being with me!

> *Come to Me, all who are weary and heavy laden,*
>
> *and I will give you rest.*
>
> *Take My yoke upon you, and learn from Me.*
>
> *For I am gentle and humble in heart;*
>
> *and you shall find rest for your souls.*
>
> *For My yoke is easy, and My load is light.*
>
> *--Matthew 11:28-30*

Day 93

8/9/15

My life feels absurd. It just doesn't make any sense. One day, I'm going along, then one day I am here. New place and new stuff. It's just ridiculous!

Thank You, Lord. When I look at my life, it makes no sense to me whatsoever! Thank You, Lord; it's Your life and You set things right. What seems and feels crazy and upside down, You make it straight and upright. Thank You, Lord; it's Your life!

I have directed you in the way of wisdom;

I have led you in upright paths.

When you walk, your steps will not be impeded;

and if you run, you will not stumble.

--Proverbs 4:11-12

Day 94

8/13/15

There is joy in the name of Jesus. Sometimes when my mind is spinning around, I just say "Jesus;" I know God delights in this. And it brings perspective to me. Because anything in my life seems different when compared to the sufferings of Jesus!

Thank You, Lord, for giving Your Son to die for us! Thank You that we have His suffering to remind us that You love us! Thank You for that generous gift!

He made Him,

who knew no sin to be sin on our behalf,

that we might become the righteousness of God in Him.

--2 Corinthians 5:21

Day 95

8/11/16

    I find that I have a certain amount of stuff I can endure regarding "him" each day. And then I'm just fed up! Oh, Jesus…Jesus! Please protect me!! Guard my heart… it no longer belongs to "him." My heart belongs to You alone.

    It is tough because I never wanted to stop loving "him." My brain does not seem to be able to break the attachment which You, Lord, have given me permission to walk away from! But I do want to let it go…this is vital to moving on! Help me, Lord Jesus, to navigate!

> *…so that He may establish your hearts*
>
> *without blame in holiness before our God and Father*
>
> *at the coming of our Lord Jesus with all His saints.*
>
> *--1 Thessalonians 3:13*

Day 96

4/30/16

I have been contemplating this for some time: should I give up trying to get my things back? They are just things! Should I let them go? And there is a feeling that "he" is just holding me hostage (no, "he" does not have the power to do that!) by keeping the things locked up and not letting me get them.

Oh Dear Lord, please show me clearly what to do. I do not want to cling to the things of this world, as to make an idol of them, or to exact my own vengeance. Make my path straight!

Behold, we count those blessed who endured,

you have heard of the endurance of Job

and have seen the outcome of the Lord's dealing,

that the Lord is full of compassion and merciful.

--James 5:11

Day 97

10/13/15

I have only to read a post on Facebook to start second guessing again. Thank You, Lord, for on this journey--You are with me!

In this post, the author was encouraging people to stay in their difficult marriages and to keep praying and fighting. I agree completely, and not at all, plus everything in between. Because as much as I would like to tell you the solution for your particular situation…I know each life is different!

And the Lord comes to will and work in each of our lives, as it brings glory to Him. Thank You, Lord; You made each of us separately and special in Your image. The work You are doing in us is as individually awesome as You are, and as You have made us!

Remind us not to look about and compare our journey with others, but to praise You on the path where You are leading us!

Rule #3   No one gets to say who I am but God. God says!

I will give thanks to Thee,

for I am fearfully and wonderfully made;

wonderful are Thy works,

and my soul knows it very well.

--Psalm 139:14

Day 98

10/11016

I spent the entire day worrying about a situation and praying…what to do? God provided for the need in three ways! You see, I was supposed to go to a dinner meeting at an expensive restaurant and didn't have the money to pay for my meal.

A check that I was expecting came in the mail; so I got cash, Yay! I wasn't all that keen on spending it since money is tight, but I prayed about it and felt I could go ahead.

My friend and I split a large meal to cut down on cost. When the check came, she said, "I'll get this." Wow! But, in the end, another lady in the group paid for everyone's meal. Awesome!

Thank You, Lord; it turns out that You are able to take care of me and even extra plans. You are amazing! Finances have been such a hard area for me to surrender to You. Thank You, Lord, for meeting me here and gently leading me along Your path!

Since then we have a great high priest

who has passed through the heavens,

Jesus the Son of God,

let us hold fast our confession.

For we do not have a high priest who cannot sympathize

with our weaknesses,

but one who has been tempted in all things as we are, yet without sin.

Let us therefore draw near with confidence to the throne of grace,

that we may receive mercy and grace to help in time of need.

--Hebrews 4:14-16

Day 99

8/10/16

When this first started…I had no real reference for truly hideous sin in my life. Up until then, I just had some ordinary sin to address!

Isn't it strange how we categorize sin, small, medium, large… extra-large! I guess we are really making judgments based on the consequences of sin! Interesting. The truth be told--sin really is sin. It is acting contrary to God and seeking self instead of what God wants. Each of our sins, no matter what they are, have been paid for by Jesus on the cross.

Thank You, Lord; You've given us not only forgiveness of our sin, but You also give redemption, continually transforming us. You use the consequences of our sin to bring us into a closer walk with You.

O Israel, hope in the Lord;

for with the Lord there is lovingkindness,

and with Him,

is abundant redemption.

--Psalm 130:7

Day 100

8/15/15

Each new day--a day to Praise You, Lord. I don't know what will happen next; but I know You will be with me!

There are things in my life that I can't do a thing about; things that do not make me happy! Do I try to change them, wrestle around and fix or manipulate! Do I accept them? I'm not sure!

Thank You, Lord, You can see every day stretching out in front of me. You know my heart; it belongs to You. You are orchestrating my life--I just can't see the music. The notes are escaping me! Thank you, Lord.

Rule #7 God's arm is long enough to walk with me every step. God loves!

Because Thy lovingkindness is better than life,

my lips will ever praise Thee.

So I will bless Thee as long as I live;

I will lift up my hands in Thy name.

--Psalm 63:3-4

Day 101

9/1/15

I'm in the waiting room. And I'm wondering how long it will take. It's so funny how we measure everything in minutes, hours, and days. How many days will this take?? And in order to measure, there must be a beginning and an end! I think my thinking might be…wrong!

Thank You, Lord; You gave me a sound mind, a new mind in Christ. I can walk in it. And Thank You. You are so much bigger than the finite time and space in which I'm living. You know everything; You see it all and are all powerful. Please remind me to look to You!

If then you have been raised up with Christ,

keep seeking the things above,

where Christ is seated at the right hand of God.

Set you mind on the things above,

not on the things that are on earth.

For you have died and your life is hidden with Christ in God.

--Colossians 3:1-3

Day 102

9/27/15

From my journal, December 4, 2014…last winter:

"Lord, I can see that I am spending so much time protecting myself from hurt that I am missing my life. I want to live with You! Teach me to see quickly the fiery darts!"

When we are attacked, there is a natural response to defend ourselves. We see it coming and gear up to fight the assault. I think this is a God given response--but I also think sometimes we use the wrong weapons! And we sometimes fight the wrong battles!

The battle I've had in my marriage was not about money or intimacy with "him," or even about infidelity. It was about the Lord being Lord of our lives. But somewhere along the way, we got distracted in sin. And we missed the Lord.

When I got on track with the Lord…"he" never did! Thank You, Lord, for speaking to me in a kind voice. I'm sorry I took a long time to listen and hear!

For our struggle is not against flesh and blood,

but against the rulers,

against the powers,

against the forces of wickedness in the heavenly places.

--Ephesians 6:12

Day 103

10/1/15

It's been a tough day of dodging little bullets of thoughts that are against the truth of God! I've repeated over and over again. "You love me, unconditionally. Thank You, Lord, for loving me unconditionally!"

And then the derail comes...because my trash can is full. My neighbor didn't take it to the street and he said he would. Weird! I really don't mind taking it to the street!

I don't know exactly why it felt like such a big deal. Maybe it's the stuff I've lost and the regular "ole sadness" about having to start over? I think I better just invoke:

Rule #1   Don't try to figure it out...it could hurt your brain. God knows!

Thank You, Lord; you do love me unconditionally. You know everything; nothing gets past You!

Oh, the depth of the riches both of the wisdom and knowledge of God!

How unsearchable are His judgments and unfathomable His ways!

...for from Him and through Him and to Him are all things.

To Him be the glory forever.

Amen.

--Romans 11:33 and 36

Day 104

7/14/16

God hates divorce. I hear this all the time in Christian circles. I wonder if they know how that feels.

Of course God hates divorce because He is so deeply grieved by sin, (it's what killed His Son)! And divorce is a product of sin and self--there's just no denying that.

So it's all well and good to know that God hates divorce...do we also know that God hates hatred, lying, cheating, selfishness, gluttony, murder, and even the thought of these? That's a lot of stuff!

I get it, Lord; but I want to go deeper. I don't want to focus another moment on what You hate. I want to give myself, my whole self, over to You. That's my only safe place!

Thank You, Lord; You will show me the path to walk...I can trust You!

The night is almost gone, and the day is at hand.

Let us therefore lay aside the deeds of darkness

and put on the armor of light.

Let us behave properly as in the day,

not in carousing and drunkenness,

not in sexual promiscuity and sensuality,

not in strife and jealousy.

But put on the Lord Jesus Christ,

and make no provision for the flesh in regard to its lusts.

--Roman 13:12-14

Day 105

10/11/16

For some reason going back to a place has prompted a sad feeling, ok—even mad! Why am I so mad…I have no idea!! So I end up spending the first hour trying to get calmed down. Good grief!

Rule #6   Lay down the *why*. God understands!

Lord, I will always, on this side of Your glory have times like these. You gave us these precious emotions to enjoy life with You and to train us. Please keep reminding me—the emotions show me what I'm really thinking and that allows me to bring it to You. Win, win!

Incline Thine ear to me,

rescue me quickly;

a stronghold to save me.

--Psalm 31:2

Day 106

9/19/16

There are clearly no words….again! Another move has been made which seems to put getting my share even farther away.

Oh Lord, I will trust You; I can trust You. I believe You are taking care! I will trust in You, Lord! I am held in Your mighty hands. You alone are powerful and awesome in all Your glory. You are watching.

This is not about me, or "him." This is about You and Your workings in our lives. Please keep my focus on You! You are Lord!

Praise the Lord!
How blessed is the man who fears the Lord,
who greatly delights in His commandments?
He will not fear evil tidings;
his heart is steadfast,
trusting in the Lord.
--Psalm 112:1 and 7

Day 107

2/1/16

Today, I am thankful for my sister! She knows how to put on socks! Mind you, she has many other talents and wonderful qualities--but the socks...I saw that one recently.

A couple of months ago, I broke my arm and I was in need of help with socks! She was there and what a deal. She pulls the sock on my foot; then she pulls on the end to give my toes a little wiggle room! Perfect! I know it's a little thing; but it's that type of details that make the difference when you're feeling rotten!

Thank You, Lord, for Linda who is beautiful inside and out! Thanks for caring for me in a completely awesome way!

But God will surely take care of you,

and bring you up from this land to the land which He promised...

--Genesis 50:24a

Day 108

8/16/16

If not for my mind reminding me over and over…I could just be here where I am! But I think satan wants me to live where I was, or at least somewhere on the fence. It's a spiritual battle!!

You see, satan came to kill, steal, and destroy. When we belong to Jesus, satan can no longer kill us, because we have eternal life. He can, however, steal away a joyous life of walking with God. And he can destroy our lives on earth with anger and bitterness…sin!

So I think that it's only as I walk closely with the Lord in thankfulness for who He is and all He's done for me, that I can see victory! Jesus is victorious! In Me!

How blessed are the people who know the joyful sound!

O Lord, they walk in the light of Thy countenance.

In Thy name they rejoice all the day,

and by Thy righteousness they are exalted.

--Psalm 89:15-16

Day 109

3/26/16

I understand in my mind that God made me and that this life I now live is His. So why am I wanting others and "him" to pay for the life I lost, which was never really mine in the first place??

Oh, Dear Lord, show me Your truth!

One thing I have asked from the Lord, that I shall seek;
that I may dwell in the house of the Lord all the days of my life,
to behold the beauty of the Lord
and to meditate in His temple.
For in the day of trouble He will conceal me in His tabernacle;
in the secret place of His tent He will hide me;
He will lift me up on a rock.
And now my head will be lifted up above my enemies around me,
and I will offer in His tent sacrifices with shouts of joy;
I will sing, yes, I will sing praises to the Lord.
--Psalm 27:4-6

Day 110

3/30/16

It's the day after Easter and I'm contemplating trusting the Lord. I mean that I'm realizing that I have many life patterns and which cause me to not trust Him!

This super difficult time in my life has shown me over and over many ways in which I'm not trusting Him! Learning to listen...! Thank You, Lord!

When you are in distress and all these things have come upon you,

in the latter days,

you will return to the Lord your God and listen to His voice.

For the Lord your God is a compassionate God;

He will not fail you nor destroy you

nor forget the covenant with your father which He swore to them.

--Deuteronomy 4:30-31

Day 111

5/12/16

Today I'm thankful for Cookie Cutters that aren't really what they seem…like a Bat reshaped to make Yoda, a Tulip that makes Darth Vader, and a Coffin that makes Pill Cookies for a graduating Nurse! Isn't this so much like walking with the Lord…nothing like I envisioned, but still so sweet! Thank You, Lord, You are so awesome!

> *Instead of a thorn bush the cypress will come up;*
> *And instead of the nettle the myrtle will come up:*
> *And it will be a memorial to the Lord,*
> *For an everlasting sign which will not be cut off.*
>
> *--Isaiah 55:13*

Day 112

8/20/16

I want to tell you the secret of the Christian life…three words: Thank You, Lord. When you practice saying these, even when you don't feel thankful, they make changes in you!

What's really happening is that you are allowing God to come into every part of your life and He is showing You who He really is. He is trustworthy, kind, wise, longsuffering, loving, and has completely sacrificed Himself for us!

When a circumstance meets our day we can say, "Thank You, Lord." Thank You, Lord, for the flat tire. Today I got out of my car, started to unload groceries and heard the hissing of my tire. Thinking I could drive to the tire place; I quickly put the groceries in the fridge. The tire went flat just as I drove in the parking lot. There was a huge hole so I needed a new tire. I had a warranty, got the new tire free and just paid $11.48 for new warranty. While I was waiting for my tire to be changed, I had an asthma attack from rubber tire smell so; I went outside to enjoy the cool, cloudy day. Sitting outside, I met an amazing homeless lady. They finished with my tire more quickly than expected, Yay!

Because I took moments to be thankful for God's provision over and over in this, He showed me all He was doing. I didn't get perturbed; I'm so thankful, He kept me from being stranded on the street, etc.!!

Oh give thanks to the Lord, call upon His name;

make known His deeds among the peoples.

Sing to Him, sing praises to Him;

speak of all His wonders.

Glory in His holy name;

let the heart of those who seek Him be glad.

--1 Chronicles 16:8-10

Day 113

8/29/16

I'm settling in to the realization that what God directed me to do that day and so many days afterwards…was to love my husband. To love him so much that I stepped out in truth and faith. There is no greater love than to lay down your own life!

That day I laid down my life and also my very hopes and dreams of a loving marriage. Instead, I chose to live and walk with Jesus and to hold to the hope that Jesus would redeem my life by making it into something truly beautiful.

I can easily say now, that He has given me a beautiful, new life. But I'm sad to say that my husband has not chosen life… this was always a possibility. God gives us free will to choose; we can choose for ourselves but can NEVER make a choice for another person! And even though this is painful, I know God is always working! Thank You, Lord; I can trust You to keep working in each of us!

For even though they knew God,

they did not honor Him as God or give thanks,

but they became futile in their speculations,

and their foolish heart was darkened.

Professing to be wise, they became fools.

--Romans 1:21-22

Day 114

9/13/16

Today I was thinking that "he" is out in the world--unable to tell the truth. And so I pray for those who cross "his" path. I've prayed many times now, that "his" lying footprint will not wreck any more lives. I pray for protection and grace for the people around "him." And that God will use the garbage for good!

Thank You, Lord! You are a redeemer! And what happens around us is Your business, not ours.

No man can by any means redeem his brother,

or give to God a ransom for him--

for the redemption of his soul is costly,

and he should cease trying forever—

that he should live on eternally;

that he should not see the pit.

--Psalm 49:7-9

Day 115

10/30/16

Oh Lord, I have not lost hope. I still believe in the sanctity of marriage. I still believe that some are able to have a loving and real marriage relationship. It's not that I believe it's all rosy; I know some days are far from it. But the 'marrieds' are surviving through Your grace!

Thank You, Lord! Thank You for showing us Your faithfulness. There is hope to be seen in every person who is following You!

And hope does not disappoint,

because the love of God has been poured out within our hearts

through the Holy Spirit who was given to us.

--Romans 5:5

Day 116

6/16/16

Let's talk trash...

Rule #3   No one gets to say who I am but God. God says!

I just happen to know what trash is; it's the fast food sack sitting in my car from my lunch on the run today. It's what's in my big blue can that will be on the curb Tuesday morning and maybe the junk mail on my table.

To contrast... it's not a person, not even someone you don't agree with, like or know. It's not you or me. And not one person on this planet can say it's so. No one gets to define you or me based on what they think!!

Only God gets to say! And He has spoken...when He sent His Son to die for us! He says, "These are my children, I made them in My image, I love them, they are My precious babies!! My treasures!" Thank You, Lord, for showing me the difference today...between trash and treasure... I'm the treasure! Sweet!

I will give thanks to Thee,

for I am fearfully and wonderfully made;

wonderful are Thy works,

and my soul knows it very well.

--Psalm 139:14

Day 117

6/1/16

Maybe a part of why I keep coming back to this stuff over and over again is that I never got to say to "him," "WHY?" Oh Dear Lord, would it make any difference? Please show me what to do about this. I would like to close the door. May I close the door?

Is it my job to do anything? Does a door need to be closed? We live everyday with relationships stringing along behind us. They're in various states--happy, harmonious, apathetic, frustrating, bitter-- please, must I go on?

And if, while I am in this Thankful Journey with You, these things are living, breathing things, have I more to do, than just to be thankful? I am thankful that You are with me, and I with You. I am thankful for Your power to work, even when I try to take over??

Thank You, Lord; I can trust You again!

He who is holy,

who is true, who has the key of David,

who opens and no one will shut,

and who shuts and no one opens, says this:

"I know your deeds.

Behold, I have put before you an open door which no one can shut,

because you have a little power, and have kept My word,

and have not denied My name."

Behold, I will cause those of the synagogue of Satan,

who say they are Jews, and are not,

but lie--behold, I will make them to come and bow down

at your feet,

and to know that I have loved you.

--Revelation 3:7b-9

Rule #8   **God, indeed, has more power that everyone and everything. God is!**

Day 118

10/18/15

I have been waiting and waiting for the Lord to bring down justice on my (still not yet) former spouse. I wouldn't seek vengeance myself, but I surely want the Lord to do something!

But today--I can see!

Rule #4   God will show you what you need to see. God sees!

Thank You, Lord, for showing me that You are the judge of the earth. That my spouse will reap according to Your statutes. Thank You, Lord, for showing me that my part is to look to You alone! I am to focus on You; not what is behind or what is ahead. Nor am I to focus on what is now, but to glance at the world around me and to gaze on You!

Though the wicked is shown favor,

he does not learn righteousness;

he deals unjustly in the land of unrighteousness,

And does not perceive the majesty of the Lord.

--Isaiah 26:10

Day 119

4/22/16

One thought that has gone with me throughout this journey is that there is a huge difference in my life when I just tell the truth. The truth does not require any forethought or prior planning. As people say these days, "It is what it is!"

When you are in a situation filled with conflict, it can be easy to get swept up and find yourself exaggerating or even lying. Stop! The truth wins! You may not see the win today, tomorrow or ever. But go for the win!

The Lord loves us, and the most important thing to Him is our being conformed more and more to His image. That's the true win. And we can't be conformed to His image when we are following after our own stuff!

Thank You, Lord, for the true win!

Rule #7   God's arm is long enough to walk with us every step. God loves!

Then the Lord answered Job out of the storm, and said,

"Now gird up your loins like a man;

I will ask you, and you instruct Me.

Will you really annul My judgment?

Will you condemn Me that you may be justified?

Or do you have an arm like God?

And can you thunder with a voice like His?"

--Job 40:6-9

Day 120

7/25/15

I am completely tired of trying to figure it out…

Rule #1   Don't try to figure it out…it could hurt your brain. God knows!

I'm spending so much energy trying to make a crazy, unreasonable situation make sense! And I can see now that this "figuring out process" has affected more than my brain! It has weighed down my soul, distracting me from being with the Lord. It has exhausted my body, keeping me up nights in sheer exasperation.

Thank You, Lord; I can clearly see that it is not my job to figure out what has happened. My part is to be with You, moment by moment! Thank You, Lord.

Thus says the Lord, "Let not a wise man boast of his wisdom,

and let not the mighty man boast of his might,

let not a rich man boast of his riches;

but let him who boasts boast of this: that he understands and knows Me,

that I am the Lord who exercises

lovingkindness, justice, righteousness on earth;

for I delight in those things."

declares the Lord!

--Jeremiah 9:23-24

Day 121

6/23/15

It was a really big step for me to get a storage space. The lawyer advised me to take things from our home. These things were mine before we were married. I didn't want to; I wanted to stay married. But "he" wanted someone else!

So I went. The bent over man was sweet. We rode a golf cart to the very end of the lockers and he said, "This is a good one for you." I said, "Yes, it is a good one." And I thought, "most of my life will be in this 10 x 10 foot space".

As we were riding back to the office, I looked up and saw: 954, 953, 952… "What's the number of that space?" I asked. Les said, "957." It gave me a big smile!!

Thank You, Lord; You know I like 5's and 7's. Those have been big numbers in my life, not magical, just part of my story. It was a little reminder from the Lord that He sees everything and cares about the smallest detail…He knows us!

Thank You Lord, You know the numbers of our days. You see each one…

So teach us to number our days,

that we may present to You a heart of wisdom.

--Psalm 90:12

Day 122

8/29/15

I feel like I don't have any answers anymore! I am fresh out, done and have no idea what to do next. This might be my personal low of all times! Jesus, Jesus, Jesus!

Thank You, Lord, I have been stopped in my tracks. I cannot go forward; I most certainly cannot go backward. Thank You, Lord; there is nothing but the here and now.

Rule #5 God's time is perfect. God endures!

If then you cannot do even a very little thing,

why are you anxious about other matters?

But if God arrays the grass in the fields,

which is alive today and tomorrow is thrown into the furnace,

how much more will He clothe you,

O men of little faith!

--Luke 12:26 and 28

Day 123

9/17/15

I'm having such a tough time getting up in the mornings. I know I must be a little depressed, sad, lonely, and confused!

Dear Lord, please remind me every morning what You have done for me! Bring to my mind Your reason for my life, Your purpose in my suffering and Your joy in my heart!

I will give thanks to Thee,

for I am fearfully and wonderfully made;

wonderful are Thy works,

and my souls knows it very well.

--Psalm 139:14

Day 124

4/17/16

As I pray over the list of my possessions--things I would like to have but cannot get--I realize that I am so angry. Not only for these but for the really big thing that "he" took away from me...our marriage! I am using too much energy focusing on the anger at not being able to get my things. I'm afraid I am missing the real root of it all!

It is easy enough to go about reliving all of the hurt but difficult to lay down my life, myself...and to rely on the Lord... Thank You, Lord, for dying for me, for bearing all the pain, and shame. You felt it all! Things are just things; even a marriage is just a relationship...but You...You are to be the most essential, important thing in my life.

In this you greatly rejoice,

even though now for a little while, if necessary,

you have been distressed by various trials,

that the proof of your faith,

being more precious than gold which is perishable,

even though tested by fire,

may be found to result in praise and glory

and honor at the revelation of Jesus Christ.

--1 Peter 1:6-7

Day 125

10/2/16

For what seems like forever, I have known about the possibility that I will get nothing of my share…half, Ha Ha! And I have wrestled with that idea. A lot!!

It's not really about the money, (although I could certainly use the money)! I know God is going to meet my needs; He has over and over!

And the stuff, some of it I could really use but I have survived this long without it. I know God will bring me what I need! Thank You, Lord.

I think what's really bothering me about the whole thing is the justice! I still want justice. I still want "him" to pay, and I want "him" to stop winning! It seems like "he" won!! And I feel like "he's" trying to manipulate me, by keeping my things--aww…I hate that feeling!!

Lord, these are a lot of mixed up ideas that I need You to straighten out in my head. I don't want to be in bondage to my ex-husband. I want to walk with You alone, not dragging a bunch of garbage behind me! Help me, Lord!

"Remember this, and be assured;

recall it to mind, you transgressors.

Remember the former things long past,

for I am God, and there is no other;

I am God, and there is no one like Me,

declaring the end from the beginning,

and from ancient times things which have not been done,

saying, 'My purpose will be established,

And I will accomplish all My good pleasure';
"*Truly I have spoken; truly I will bring it to pass.*
I have planned it, surely I will do it."
--Isaiah 46:8-10, 11b

Day 126

3/26/16

I have been struck this week (Easter 2016) by how God is obligated by His own character to care for us.

He willingly made Himself not only our Savior, but committed His whole existence to us, His children. He can be none other than who He is, our caregiver, our helper, the one who loves us! And yet, I'm all absorbed in myself…may His praise always be on my lips!!

He made Himself who knew no sin to be sin on our behalf,

that we might become the righteousness of God in Him.

--2 Corinthians 5:21

Day 127

6/28/15

Will I ever stop feeling/being tied to "him?" I can't stand it! Maybe it's because I feel so out of control of this situation? But the very thought of it...feels BAD!

"He" left me...my brain is not catching up with that idea! Thank You, Lord, I can cry out to You and You hear!

Hear, O Lord, when I cry with my voice,

and be gracious to me and answer me."

--Psalm 27:7

Day 128

9/28/16

On Sunday, my life group leader sent me on a trip in my memory. He didn't mean to, but when he mentioned the word 'whetstone' in an example...there I went!

I used to have a whetstone. It was in a wooden base, and sat on the hearth at our house. It belonged to my dad; he would use it to sharpen knives. And he's been gone since 2000.

I say I used to have it, because it was one of the many things I left behind. There were some days when I could get into the house after I left my husband of 18 years. I had begun to take some of my things. Then there was the one day, moving out of big stuff...I figured I would be locked out after that and I was!

The whetstone was a small thing that I missed taking. It reminds me that I have lost many things, including my marriage!

Thank You, Lord, I have not lost You; that's the most important thing! And I have not lost my memories of my dad! And thanks for reminding me that things are just things; but You, You are with me forever!

My soul, wait in silence for God only,

for my hope is from Him.

He only is my rock and my salvation,

my stronghold;

I shall not be shaken.

--Psalm 62:5-6

Day 129

6/28/15

I remember the day I left. I couldn't stop shaking! I had no idea what would happen. I'm living in it and I still have no idea what's happening!

But I know something; God has traveled with me each step. He has protected me, guided me, loved me, and shown Himself to me! Thank You, Lord!

Teach me Thy way, O Lord,

and lead me in the level path,

because of my foes.

--Psalm 27:11

Day 130

7/30/15

I have been practicing spending time with the Lord before anything! It so easy to jump out of bed, running after everything that needs to be done! In fact, I can often start thinking of things while I'm waking up. But the Lord has convinced me that He wants me first, to direct me and to give me a clear focus for the day!

So I sit, pray, read a devotional, read God's word and sometimes post a favorite verse on Facebook…after I've spent this time with the Lord!

Thank You, Lord, for direction and focus. Thank You for meeting me in the morning! And for meeting me all throughout my, Your day!

As for me, I shall call upon God,

and the Lord will save me.

Evening and morning and at noon,

I will complain and murmur,

and He will hear my voice.

He will redeem my soul in peace,

from the battle which is against me,

for they are many who strive with me.

--Psalm 55:16-18

Day 131

8/18/15

A part of me really wants "him" to continue in sin. That way I can continue to hate "him." I can wallow in the anger and bitterness, and no one can blame me for that--right?

Dear Lord, Thank You for showing me my heart and my thinking. Please keep me near to You!

Thank You--You can unpack these intense feelings and make sense of them. You are completely able to lead me through forgiveness. You will protect my heart from bitterness and rage. You understand all of it and are not afraid! Lord, I surrender this to You; You alone are Holy!

This is the covenant that I will make with them

after those days, says the Lord:

'I will put my laws upon their heart,

and upon their mind I will write them.'

He then says,

'And their sins and their lawless deeds

I will remember no more.'

--Hebrews 10:16-17

Day 132

9/12/15

Bit by bit...thinking about "him" and our life together is going away. And I'm starting to lay down the past and step into my future with the Lord.

It helps if I practice punctuating my sentences with... 'But God!' My mind races, 'But God' is able! My words are about my loss, 'But God' redeems! Some days I do well at this practice, some days--not so much!

Thank You, Lord; You are teaching me day by day to walk with You. Thank You, Lord, for speaking to me!

And your ears will hear a word behind you,

'this is the way, walk in it.'

Whenever you turn to the right or to the left.

--Isaiah 30:21

Day 133

10/6/15

It's funny because when I'm in a good time, I'm looking around, wondering when the next bad time will come. I know it will come!

When I mentioned this to my friend… "What if the bad thing happens?" She laughed, "You're joking, right? You're already in the bad thing!"

Thank You, Lord, You have made the bad thing bearable. You have carried me so many times, through the last two years and the last seven months. And You will carry me through the next…however long!

Surely our griefs He Himself bore,

and our sorrows He carried:

yet we ourselves esteemed Him stricken,

smitten of God, and afflicted.

--Isaiah 53:4

Day 134

8/22/15

We are not supposed to walk in fear in rain or shine or anything else! Fear is not from the Lord! I can't even think how many times I have seen, 'do not fear' in the bible!

And when I realize I am in the fear, I can know instantly that I am believing a lie. It is a lie about who God is, or who I am in Christ.

Thank You, Lord; the recognizing is getting faster. Thank You for this awesome foundational truth in my walk with You!

But as for me,

the nearness of God is my good;

I have made the Lord God my refuge,

that I may tell of all Thy works.

--Psalm 73:28

Day 135

7/4/15

I believe that God knows everything and that He is truth, He speaks things into being, and He says I am His precious child. He endures throughout time and understands me, and He loves me. Since I believe these things, how can I ever believe I am alone, left abandoned, lied to, uncared for, unloved, misunderstood, and basically worthless??

These two beliefs cannot exist together; it would be as if I had two heads that are in a battle! So, as I walk more closely with Him, I am seeing, learning, laying down, and weighing thoughts against truth and always in the process of being transformed. I am new and always being made new, walking in the newness of life!

Thank You, Lord, for Your beautiful redemptive work in us! Thank You that I can trust You each moment!

And do not be conformed to this world,

but be transformed by the renewing of your mind,

that you may prove what the will of God is,

that which is good and acceptable and perfect.

--Romans 12:2

Day 136

6/19/15

It is one thing to apply reasoning to a situation, come to a conclusion, and then say "Okay, Lord, I know You're working it out!" It's another thing altogether to say before the reasoning, "Lord, I cannot, will not, figure this out; I will trust You for all of it, top to bottom!" Thank You, Lord; You are completely capable of taking care of me, Your Baby!

> *But He led forth His own people like sheep*
> *and guided them in the wilderness like a flock;*
> *He led them safely, so that they did not fear;*
> *But the sea engulfed their enemies.*
>
> *--Psalm 78:52-53*

Day 137

7/6/15

Without realizing, I am carrying a judging spirit. I am constantly getting onto myself for doing something "wrong." I know this is from years of wrong thinking about how capable I am to run my own life. And of course by default, how God must not be able to help me!

Thank You, Lord; You are showing me this every day. I know You want to do so, You will and You are able to come against any lie I am believing.

Your desire is to gently expose (although, sometimes painfully) these lies. And Your desire also is to bring me to the truth. Lord, help me camp in the truth and lay down the lies!!

Lead me in Thy truth and teach me;
for Thou are the God of my salvation;
for Thee I wait all the day.
--Psalm 25:5

Day 138

7/7/15

How can this latest thing be a gift from God? Can it be that God knew today would happen? Can it be that He is not surprised? Is He planning to be standing by, leaning closer to touch my pain and give it a healing balm?

Thank You, Lord; I know it's true, please hold me up here, while my joy is gone. Please bring peace where there is panic. Be power and might and glory and majesty and victory in me!

Thine, O Lord is the greatness,

and the power and the glory and the victory and the majesty,

indeed everything that is in the heavens and the earth,

Thine is the dominion, O Lord,

and Thou dost exalt Thyself as head of all.

--1 Chronicles 29:11

Day 139

7/8/15

There is much glory in trusting the Lord! There have been countless times this year when a situation made me want to scream and cry and lash out. But, when I have practiced thanking the Lord for it and waiting on Him, there was so much peace afterwards!

These emotions that the Lord has given us--I know He wants to use them for His glory. Thank You, Lord, for showing me Your truth when the emotions come! They can show what I'm really thinking and believing about You and who I am in You!

All discipline for the moment seems not to be joyful, but sorrowful;

yet to those who are trained by it,

afterwards it yields the peaceful fruit of righteousness.

--Hebrews 12:11

Day 140

7/8/15

Rule #7   God's arm is long enough to walk with me every step. God loves!

There is a big difference between an imagined betrayal and real betrayal. I think the pain of it, when imagined, is so huge. There is so much room for more imagining, but there is still hope that it is not true.

Once you know the betrayal is real, has happened and is happening…then you are in different place. There are real consequences!!

Thank You, Lord; You met me when I only thought my husband was breaking our marriage. You walked alongside me each day in each new thing. You were there to encourage me to trust You and wait (the hardest thing ever!). And Thank You, Lord; You are walking with me now that I know the truth of the situation. You have been in so many details, orchestrating my life into a beautiful song of glory and grace.

For the Lord God is a sun and shield;

the Lord gives grace and glory;

no good thing does He withhold from those who walk uprightly.

O Lord of hosts;

how blessed is the man who trusts in Thee!

--Psalm 84:11-12

Day 141

8/19/16

Even though "he" took away our relationship, our life together, our marriage, "he" cannot ever take away all of the things that You, Lord, did in my life during our marriage! The ways that You have been faithful to me, the truth You have shown me, brothers and sisters in Christ, sweet fellowship, growing in the Lord—those can never be taken away by any man or circumstance!

Thank You, Lord; You have met me over and over; You have shown Yourself and rescued me to carry me here. Thank You for this wonderful place where I am; Thank You, Lord.

God is faithful,

through whom you were called into fellowship with His Son,

Jesus Christ our Lord.

--1 Corinthians 1:9

Day 142

10/2/15

How often I wake up with the expectation of not thinking of "him." My brain says, "Don't think about "him." It is similar to a "wet paint, don't touch" sign… When I am concentrating so hard on not doing something, often, that is what I do!

Thank You, Lord. You have given me many things to think about instead of obsessing on the details of my divorce. I have only to look around Your world to see You in all Your glory!!

And one called out to another and said,

"Holy, Holy, Holy, is the Lord of hosts,

the whole earth is full of His glory."

--Isaiah 6:3

Day 143

9/29/16

It seems that I have hit another wall, a trusting wall. So, the question is, "How far down into the valley will I go with You, Lord--How far away from where I think I should be will I let You lead me?"

And while You are leading me, will I listen to the darty thoughts? "See, He doesn't really love you, He's just toying with you. God's not really going to take care of you!"

No matter what, Lord, I will follow You--go ahead and lead me away from the direction I think I should be going. Lead me away from what looks only like heaven; I will follow You.

I will wait for You even when it seems like You have left me. I will wait. I will wait here when it seems that You have left me--until You tell me what to do next!

I wait for the Lord, my soul does wait,

and in His word, do I hope.

My soul waits for the Lord more that the watchman for the morning;

indeed, more that the watchman for the morning.

--Psalm 130:5-6

Day 144

1/23/16

It's been a tough day. I had to deal with an unhappy person; she wasn't pleased with some cookies I made. So I was able to practice walking with the Lord in the midst of it!

It can be easy to quickly defend yourself and attack the other person. But I didn't want to do that. Even though the solution I offered was not what she had in mind, I certainly did not want to lash out at and be the "winner." What I wanted to do was honor the Lord, give grace to the person and to make certain to entrust myself to the Lord!

Thank You, Lord; in You there is victory. I can rely on You to walk with me. I can stop and ask You what to do. I can check-in with You about the details. And I can wait for a response about what to do next!

Behold, Thou dost desire truth in the innermost being.

And in the hidden part Thou wilt make me know wisdom.

--Proverbs 51:6

Day 145

8/1/16

The truth is…words to live by today!

So many little darty thoughts come at us every day. We must keep holding up the truth in the face of them. Or they may take root in our hearts and become a fortress against Go and against us.

Thank You, Lord; You are able to show me the truth each time. Please let truth shine in me!

Rule #2   Don't dialogue with the devil. God is truth!

Finally, brethren, whatever is true, whatever is honorable,

whatever is right, whatever is pure,

whatever is lovely, whatever is of good repute,

if there is any excellence and if anything worthy of praise,

let your mind dwell on these things.

The things you have learned and received and heard and seen in me,

practice these things;

and the God of peace shall be with you.

--Philippians 4:8-9

Day 146

8/11/16

This whole time, I have had this overwhelming feeling that "he" cannot pay for the wrong "he" has done.

And up against that...Jesus, saw, knew, knows, and has paid for, this sin! For me, today, that will be enough. Jesus paid it all...

Thank You, Lord; I put my trust in You. You love justice and mercy. I can trust You even when someone has wronged me. You are still working. I surrender any right I think I have to get revenge. And I rest in You!

Righteousness and justice are the foundation of Thy throne;

lovingkindness and truth go before Thee.

--Psalm 89:14

Day 147

2/6/16

It's a sweet thing when in the difficult place, I get a little laugh from the Lord. I have been attacked again this week by the one I loved. It has been hard…

Rule #2 Don't dialogue with the devil. God is truth!

I've been reminded again that God only tells the truth! And His people seek to walk in the truth, just like me! Confusion and fear are in the lies!

So the little laugh…"he" claimed to have a heart attack (info sent to a third party in an email). Only "he" spelled it 'heart attract,' Yep, "he" had a 'heart attract,' "his" heart was attracted to someone else…slip of the tongue, I think?

Thank You, Lord; even in the midst of this barrage of lies, I can see a little humor. I can rejoice that You are truth! And I can even see this with a lot less "sting" than I have all year!

What is desirable in a man is his kindness,

and it is better to be a poor man than a liar!

--Proverbs 19:22

Day 148

3/27/15

Spontaneous crying seems to mostly happen in my car. I'll be going along and thoughts are firing through my mind. And even though I'm taking thoughts captive, "You have over-reacted, they were just friends." Vs...Lord, You love me, I am Your precious child. You showed what was really happening with "him" and "her."

Even then, sometimes the pain in my heart overwhelms me and there is anguish in my soul. Tears start to come...and I let them. It's raw and real and I don't want to keep that pain away from You, Lord; I want to give it to You! There's a comfort place with You. Thank You, Lord; You are the great, awesome comforter of Your babies!

Blessed be the God and Father of our Lord Jesus Christ,

the Father of mercies,

and God of all comfort;

who comforts us in all our affliction

so that we may be able to comfort those who are in any affliction

with the comfort with which we ourselves are comforted by God.

--2 Corinthians 1:3-4

Day 149

7/22/15

Even today…when I'm moving out of a friend's home where I've been staying for four months, and moving into my own new place, even today, I'm asking why??

Rule #1   Don't try to figure it out…it could hurt your brain. God knows!

I can't camp here—but it seems like all the work the Lord has been doing just went away today. And I'm back where I started six months ago!

Oh Dear Lord, Thank You; You know everything! You were there when "he" took the first small step to leave our marriage. You saw all the other steps; plus You were there with me for my steps toward You and this new life You're building in me.

Thank You for being ever present and never absent from me! I love You, Lord!

Humble yourselves, therefore,

under the mighty hand of God,

that He may exalt you at the proper time,

casting all your anxiety upon Him,

because He cares for you.

--1 Peter 5:6-7

Day 150

7/26/15

Again, again with the questioning! How many times will I wonder during this process of going through divorce--will I have this discussion with myself?

Rule #2   Don't dialogue with the devil. God is truth!

Dear Lord, Thank You! You tell the truth! You love me; You take care of me. You will never leave me. You are beautiful to me!

Teach me to do Thy will,

for Thou are my God;

let Thy good Spirit lead me on level ground.

For the sake of Thy name, O Lord, revive me.

In Thy loving-kindness cut off my enemies,

and destroy all those who afflict my soul:

for I am Thy servant.

--Psalm 143:10-12

Day 151

10/9/15

    I have been trying to figure out what to do with the seventeen and half years of marriage. Do I throw it all out? There is just no way. To assume it was all bad and for nothing would be to say that God wasn't there. And He most assuredly was with me all the while.

    Thank You, Lord; You walked with me through those places. You held me up and spoke to me and through me so many times! You never left me in the darkest of days. Thank You, Lord!!

Give thanks to the Lord,

for He is good;

for His lovingkindness is everlasting.

--Psalm 136:1

Day 152

3/25/16

I have not been able to write for a while—not because I am too busy, but because no words will come. Maybe I'm just scared about court; it's only two weeks away.

Oh Dear Jesus, please be my rest!

The Lord preserves the simple;

I was brought low, and He saved me.

Return to your rest, O my soul,

for the Lord has dealt bountifully with you.

For Thou hast rescued my soul from death,

my eyes from tears,

my feet from stumbling.

I shall walk before the Lord

in the land of the living.

--Psalm 116:6-9

Day 153

7/22/15

I catch myself holding back—I guess a little afraid to move forward! Even though I know You have clearly shown me this new place to go…I might be happy on some level? I am trusting You each step I see! But I am still holding back in my heart!

Thank You, Lord, for showing me Your way in my life. Thank you for being ever present! Thank You for whispering to my spirit and for presenting sweet details before me like little pebbles on my path. Thank You for Your great attention to detail!

Rule #5   God's time is perfect. God endures!

And your ear will hear a word behind you.

"This is the way, walk in it,"

whenever you turn to the right or the left.

--Isaiah 30:21

Day 154

7/22/15

This is a big thing--moving into a place of my own! And it's taken me until now just to realize that it is so big. And maybe I was thinking in the back of my mind that "he" would ride in and say, "Not really, we should stay together and work it out" …just kidding. I can't even write this without laughing out loud!

There have been so many changes--exhausting! Maybe this is what the Lord was revealing a couples of days ago, when I realized that my husband left and is living with a woman and they are not married. It sounded so ridiculous a thought at the time--I know "he's" with "her!" But deep down—the Lord was showing me that I'm still holding onto that guy…even though "he" is completely out from under the sweet umbrella of God's protection. The umbrella, that special space that we live in when we are walking with the Lord, yielded to Him!

Thank You, Lord, for gently showing me just what I need to see and when I should see it! Thank You for being faithful and wise!

Rule #4   God will show you what you need to see. God sees!

…each man's work will become evident;

for the day will show it,

because it is to be revealed with fire;

and the fire itself will test the quality of each man's work.

--1 Corinthians 3:13

Day 155

7/23/15

When I look back over the last few months, I can see the places where my choice was to act out in anger and vengeance or to allow the Lord to act on my behalf. Each time there was a fine line. And each time there was a sweet reward for obeying the Lord. That sweet reward is, knowing Him more!

While my friends would often want to err on the side of seeking retribution, the Lord kept bringing to mind one thought: when I stand before Him at the beginning of eternity—what will I have to give Him? And I just keep thinking, "I want to bring You myself, Your child, without the extra baggage!"

So that's what I sought to do. But even yesterday, I found myself second guessing--should have, could have, would have!

Thank You, Lord, for each of those opportunities to follow You. Thank You for the prompting to lay down self and walk in Your love!

For the Lord gives wisdom;

from His mouth come knowledge and understanding.

He stores up sound wisdom for the upright;

He is a shield to those who walk in integrity,

guarding the paths of justice,

and He preserves the way of His godly ones.

--Proverbs 2:6-8

Day 156

7/26/15

I find myself caught in a whirlwind of doubt and uncertainty. I would really like to leave it behind for good…could I, Lord?

I'm exhausted from worry over what 'he" keeps doing to hurt me. I would like to be rid of that for good…may I, Lord?

I want to be free from questioning everything about my life…will I, Lord?

Thank You, Lord; I am Yours; You are leading me. You have a plan for me. Your plan is to walk with me each step. Up, down, this way or that, You will not fall asleep—You see it all!

Thank You, Lord; I can count on You no matter what happens in the world!

Though youths grow weary and tired,

and vigorous young men stumble badly,

yet those who wait for the Lord,

will gain new strength;

they will mount up with wings like eagles,

they will run and not get tired,

they will walk and not become weary.

--Isaiah 40:30-31

Day 157

11/12/15

There will come a time when you are in the middle…despair will visit you, as never before. "How am I going to live, what am I going to do?"

Stop as soon as you realize that the voices are bombarding you. And say, "Thank You, Lord, this actually feels worse than all the other bad stuff before! But God, I know You are working. I know You have a plan which is the good, smart and perfect plan for me! Thank You, Lord!"

> *"For I know that plans that I have for you"* declares the Lord,
>
> *"plans for welfare and not for calamity*
>
> *to give you a future and a hope."*
>
> *--Jeremiah 29:11*

Day 158

7/23/15

Some days it really is three steps forward and two steps back! For example, I moved into my own place after five long months in limbo. Yeah! Then I discovered "he" cancelled my health insurance, (against the court order), and the cold water won't turn off in the kitchen! Laughing out loud!

Thank You, Lord; I knew how to turn off the water under the sink! And Thank You, Lord, that I don't really have to measure my life or success by anything—only to keep my eyes on You. My life is Your business—You are working here. Thank You for being with me in good or bad—it's all for Your glory!

Rule #7   God's arm is long enough to walk with me every step! God loves!

Behold, the Lord's hand is not so short that it cannot save;

neither is His ear so dull that it cannot hear.

--Isaiah 59:1

Day 159

7/28/15

Rule #1   Don't try to figure it out…it could hurt your brain. God knows!

I seem to be here again…trying to understand why this person is acting needlessly cruel to me! Why would "he" do this? I have tried my best to follow the Lord's leading, actually practicing a kind attitude toward "him." But to no avail!

Thank You, Lord; there are no answers! So I must rest in You. I'm waiting for Your word and Your help. Please show me what to do next. Please heal my wounded heart.

Thank You, Lord; You know everything. You know what "he's" going to do next! And You will guide me through that too! I love You, Lord!

Therefore, since Christ has suffered in the flesh,

arm yourselves also with the same purpose,

because he who has suffered in the flesh has ceased from sin.

So as to live the rest of the time in the flesh no longer for the lusts of men,

but for the will of God.

--1 Peter 4:1-2

Day 160

7/28/15

Today, I went to a laundromat—that's what we call them in Oklahoma where I live! I had been dreading it for a week; but since the Lord provided a place to live with no laundry, off I went!

I usually hate new things or anything I haven't done in a while. It's been years, probably since college, that I left home to do my washing! Anyway…Thank You, Lord; it wasn't scary at all. A sweet little lady helped me, and I allowed myself to not be perfect or completely knowledgeable. I might just go back there again and make some new relationships! Thank You, Lord, for going before and behind us each step!

For He will give His angels charge concerning you,

to guard you in all your ways.

They will bear you up in their hands,

lest you strike your foot against a stone.

--Psalm 91:11-12

Day 161

8/2/15

This week has been a time of heaviness and doubt. What if...should I go back? What if...?

O Dear Lord, Thank You. Even when I am unsure how to go forward, You are with me! When I am afraid, You are with me. When my world is messy, You are with me. Thank You, Lord; You comfort me and care for me and You are big enough.

But thanks be to God,

who always leads us in His triumph in Christ,

and manifests through us the sweet aroma of the knowledge

of Him in every place.

--2 Corinthians 2:14

Rule #7 God's arm is long enough to walk with me every step. **God loves!**

Day 162

8/3/15

I found great joy today, sitting in the laundry, watching my clothes spin around in the washer. There were some bright colors in every load; they looked beautiful!

Thank You, Lord, for the beauty and magnificence of You that is everywhere. Thank You that I'm home tonight with clean clothes. Thank You that You are helping me, bit by bit to put things in order. And it's an order of Your design. Thank You for providing special work to do, services to perform, food, and clothing for each of Your babies. Thanks for meeting needs.

And my God shall supply all your needs

according to His riches in glory in Christ Jesus.

--Philippians 4:19

Day 163

8/24/15

It is so difficult, to see that "he" seems to be getting away with bad things, time after time. "He" just does the bad things to me and it seems as though no one even notices!

Thank You, Lord; You notice. You have not missed a thing! You see it all. Thank You, Lord; You are with me and You are comforting me. You guide me along Your path. You will not leave me. Your truth will rescue me. I am not in the pit. I am free to walk with You!

Nevertheless I am continually with Thee;

Thou hast taken hold of my right hand.

with Thy counsel Thou wilt guide me,

and afterward receive me to glory.

--Psalm 73:23-24

Day 164

9/26/15

I'm living next door to a fairly quiet person, but he sometimes has someone stay with him, who is a "clomper." That person clomps around the house in the morning and in the night, in the middle of the night. And it is loud! It's disturbing and annoying!

Anyway, I was reading my journal from fourteen months ago and there it was…"I'm really angry with… "he" acts like a jerk, clomps around, angry, because I asked: "Please help me; I've worked sixteen hours today."

Thank You, Lord; You have a sense of humor. You are orchestrating things together over time to show me Your truths!

Let your eyes look directly ahead,

and let your gaze be fixed straight in front of you.

Watch the path of your feet.

And all your ways will be established.

Do not turn to the right nor to the left;

turn your foot from evil.

--Proverbs 4:25-27

Day 165

7/13/16

    Truly, I cannot see what will be next. Here where you are today-- its okay with the Lord. The Lord can see around the bend in your road. He's aware of every pitfall, every bump. And He is big enough for each thing ahead. And only while you're walking will you see, sometimes, what He's seeing. Maybe you'll get a tiny glimpse of Him holding you up! Thank You, Lord, for seeing!

> *Thus says the Lord,*
>
> *"Restrain your voice from weeping,*
>
> *and your eyes from tears;*
>
> *for your work shall be rewarded." declares the Lord,*
>
> *"And they shall return from the land of the enemy.*
>
> *And there is hope for your future," declares the Lord.*
>
> *--Jeremiah 31:16-17a*

Rule #4   God will show you what you need to see. God sees!

Day 166

10/7/15

Why is it, when we see a sign that says "wet paint," that we feel the need to touch it? We want to see if it is really wet, and there it is—a big yellow spot on our finger!

It's the same way with me when I focus on something in my life that is wrong... I'll just use eating for an example. God made me with a need to eat; simple, right! But I have focused on it so much for my entire life that it has become a giant issue. Don't eat that; it's not good for me. I weigh how much?!?

Please, Lord, help me focus on the main stuff and offer my life up to You. It's telling others about who You are and how much You love them. Take my focus off of my "wet paint" issues as I focus on YOU!

Thank You, Lord, for eyes to see, ears to hear, and a heart to obey!

Jesus said to them,

"My food is to do the will of Him who sent Me,

and to accomplish His work."

--John 4:34

Day 167

8/12/15

Oh, Dear Lord, I am physically exhausted! Please give me strength for the work You have given me today. Please hold me up each moment. Lord, soothe my aching muscles, my tired bones, and my stiff joints.

Thank You, Lord, for each opportunity to trust You with my day. Please keep my mind sharp—to meet each attack of satan! Remind me of the truth to hold up against each fiery dart. Lord, You are strong!

> *How blessed is the man whose strength is in Thee;*
>
> *in whose heart are the highways to Zion!*
>
> *Passing through the valley of Baca,*
>
> *they make it a spring;*
>
> *the early rain also covers it with blessings.*
>
> *They go from strength to strength,*
>
> *every one of them appears before God in Zion.*
>
> *--Psalm 84:5-7*

Rule #7   God's arm is long enough to walk with me every step. God loves!

Day 168

11/4/15

My counselor keeps saying to me, "You've been through some bad stuff." I think, "Yes, I have!" Sometimes I just need to say it out loud… "I have been through some bad stuff, and I need to keep walking through it!"

Still, emotions just well up. I feel sad about what I've lost. There are so many things to worry about, cry about and grieve over! But Lord, I have so many reasons to rejoice!

So, I can lay aside the sadness; allowing You to meet me there, but looking forward to the new way You are leading me.

Rejoice in the Lord always;

again I say, rejoice!

Let your forbearing spirit be known to all men,

the Lord is near.

Be anxious for nothing,

but in everything by prayer and supplication with thanksgiving,

let your requests be made known to God.

And the peace of God,

which surpasses all comprehension,

shall guard your hearts and minds in Christ Jesus.

--Philippians 4:4-7

Day 169

11/12/15

I am often tempted to believe that I have so much power over my world. This is the "self" that the Lord is dealing with in me each day!

The way I know I am thinking this lie...I begin to hear guilt and condemnation but that is most definitely not from God.

"There is therefore no condemnation for those who are in Christ Jesus."

--Romans 8:1

I begin to think that something is completely my fault (my broken marriage). I also think I have caused this catastrophic thing to happen (my home being burglarized by my druggie neighbors-- twice). It's as if I think the whole world is at my beck and call, that I have directed the universe to make other people perform these deeds. Get over yourself, girl!!

Indeed—God is in charge of the world. And He has given each person the opportunity to walk with Him or choose his/her own path. I have nothing to do with the other person's choices—not that much power!!

For those who are according to the flesh
set their minds on the things of the flesh,
but those who are according to the Spirit,
the things of the Spirit.
For the mind set on the flesh is death,
but the mind set on the Spirit is life and peace.

--Romans 8:5-6

Day 170

11/12/15

I had no idea how much courage it would take to walk through this year. Looking back I can see so many footprints where God has carried me along.

Thank You, Lord; You have met me and brought me and kept me. You are glorious and worthy of praise.

I will give thanks to the Lord with all my heart;

I will tell of all Thy wonders.

I will be glad and exult in Thee.

I will sing praise to Thy name, O Most High.

--Psalm 9:1

Day 171

4/4/16

I have been operating under the idea that I need to forget "him." This has ruled my thinking for over a year. But it almost seems as if I am even more prone to think of "him" than ever before.

What if—I'm not supposed to work to forget the one I loved? Maybe I'm supposed to walk—each moment, dependent on the Lord. And when I think of "him," I lay it at the feet of Jesus.

Thank You, Lord; I believe You are big enough for each time I think of "him." And You are always big enough to train me as I walk with You.

As for God, His way is blameless;

the word of the Lord is tried;

He is a shield to all who take refuge in Him.

for who is God, but the Lord?

And who is a rock, except our God,

the God who girds me with strength,

and makes my feet like hinds' feet,

And sets me upon my high places.

He trains my hands for battle...

--Psalm 18:30-34a

Day 172

9/13/16

Getting this Christian life right--Ha-ha--is hard. Could it be because of all the measuring?! Did I do it well enough to get someone's approval? Am I measuring up? Just the thought of getting all the pegs in the right holes—is exhausting.

Wake up, Sister, I'm not in charge of this! This is not my rodeo, not my clowns! This is God's work, His poem, and His tapestry. So, so hard to remember!

Thank You, Lord; I have only to lay my life before You each day, each moment! I can walk with You. I am amazed at all You are doing!

He who loves his life loses it;

and he who hates his life in the world

shall keep it to life eternal.

If anyone serves Me,

let him follow Me;

and where I am, there shall My servant also be;

if any one serves Me,

the Father will honor him.

--John 12:25-26

Day 173

3/30/16

Thank You, Lord; every day I wake up and do what You set before me. Please give me a glad heart. Please remind me that I'm not alone!

This life that I thought I would be sharing with "him," is not going to happen that way. Give me strength, Lord. Thank You, Lord, for today.

Strength and Dignity are her clothing,

and she smiles at the future.

--Proverbs 31:25

Day 174

8/24/16

It's been an extra rough day, so I'm just going to praise the Lord!! Thank You, Lord, for being near, for holding me in Your arms!

I'm bearing a heavy soul...the deep grief is overwhelming! When I try to interact with this one I used to be married to, even to settle things, there are only more crazy lies and angry words from "him."

Praise the Lord; You care for me!! You are walking with me through this.

Rule #7   God's arm is long enough to walk with me every step. God loves!

> *Can a throne of destruction be allied with You,*
> *one which devises mischief by decree?*
> *They band themselves together against the life of the righteous,*
> *and condemn the innocent to death.*
> *But the Lord has been my stronghold,*
> *and my God the rock of my refuge.*
> *And He has brought back their wickedness upon them,*
> *and will destroy them in their evil;*
> *the Lord, our God will destroy them.*
>
> *--Psalm 94:20-23*

Day 175

7/11/16

--Psalm 84

How lovely are Thy dwelling places, O Lord of hosts!
My soul longed and even yearned for the courts of the Lord;
my heart and my flesh sing for joy to the living God.
The bird also has found a house, and the swallow a nest for herself,
where she may lay her young.
Even Thine altars, O Lord of Hosts, My King and My God.
How blessed are those who dwell in Thy house!
They are ever praising Thee.
How blessed is the man whose strength is in Thee;
in whose heart are the highways to Zion!
Passing through the valley of Baca, they make it a spring,
the early rain also covers it with blessings.
They go from strength to strength, every one of them
appear before God in Zion.
O lord of Hosts, hear my prayer; give ear, O God of Jacob!
Behold our shield, O God,
and look upon the face of Thine anointed.
For a day in Thy courts is better than a thousand outside.
I would rather stand at the threshold of the house of my God,
than dwell in the tents of wickedness.
For the Lord God is a sun and shield; the Lord gives grace and glory;
No good thing does He withhold from those who walk uprightly.
O Lord of Hosts, how blessed is the man who trusts in Thee!

Day 176

8/31/16

There have been times, along this journey, when I have felt as if I'm turning a corner. Tonight was such a time.

Can it be that a year and a half ago, I did the kindest possible thing for my spouse? I walked away, told the truth, and have continued to tell the truth. Perhaps, forcing "him" to face the truth…as much as one can "force" another to do something?!

Thank You, Lord; Your truth sustains and directs us. You meet us in kindness and truth!

And the Lord's bond servant must not be quarrelsome,

but be kind to all,

able to teach, patient when wronged,

with gentleness correcting those who are in opposition,

if perhaps God may grant them repentance,

leading to knowledge of the truth,

and they may come to their senses and escape from the snare of the devil,

having been held captive by him to do his will.

--2 Timothy 2:24-26

Day 177

2/27/16

There has been a strong, deep truth running through my mind about the destruction of my marriage. How can "he" repay—what "he" has done to me?

The truth is—there is no way to recapture the trust. It has eroded over years of lying, deceit, hiding and denying. And to add to it, all of the things "he" has done since I left—the list is long. Though it seems weird that "he" would keep trying to destroy me when "he" is the one who has stepped into this other relationship. That is so strange to me!!

So when I try to account for the situation, it is truly clear that "he" can never repay what "he" had done. This leads me directly to the Cross! Thank You, Lord!

At the foot of the Cross, I can see that Jesus bore all of our sin on Himself. He paid the price for my sin, and the sin of this one I loved and to whom I committed my life.

After this,

Jesus knowing that all things had already been accomplished,

in order that the scripture might be fulfilled, said, "I am thirsty."

A jar full of sour wine was standing there;

so they put a sponge full of sour wine on a branch of hyssop,

and brought it to His mouth.

When Jesus had received the sour wine,

He said, "It is finished!"

And He bowed His head,

and gave up His spirit."

--John 19:28-30

Day 178

2/27/16

And next to the strong, deep truth, that Jesus paid it all, there is forgiveness. Yes, I can forgive "him" because of the work of Jesus on the Cross.

This brings me to trust. I see that I can walk in forgiveness but not trust "him!" "He" has destroyed the trust. That would have to be rebuilt, over time, if "he" ever desires to walk in truth.

And this is a matter that is way, way too big for me.

Rule #4   God will show you what you need to see. God sees!

Thank You, Lord; You have brought me here and You will show me what is next. You will hold me up—wherever You take me!

Bless our God, O peoples,

and sound His praise abroad,

who keeps us in life

and does not allow our feet to slip.

—Psalm 66:8-9

Day 179

5/25/16

I have had trouble my entire Christian life with the fact that suffering exists. Why, oh why would God allow hurt to come into the lives of the ones He loves, created and redeemed??

I think that now I have a better understanding of suffering. It's through this present suffering that I have seen His presence, His power, and His glory. And I have been changed, growing even deeper down into Him with strong roots planted in the truth. Thank You, Lord, for this growing time with You. It is so sweet!

If I have learned one thing (I've learned so many), it is that You so wisely use suffering to change lives. Amazing!

A wise man will hear and increase in learning,

and a man of understanding will acquire wise counsel,

the fear of the Lord is the beginning of knowledge;

fools despise wisdom and instruction.

--Proverbs 1:5 and 7

Day 180

10/25/16

I am amazed to still feel that I'm walking this tightrope! On one end is the former life, with all its craziness, manipulation, and lies. On the other, new life in You, Lord, is my inheritance.

And some days are filled with wanting my "things." This causes such a struggle; in order to get them, I have to come in contact with the garbage of our devastated relationship.

Thank You, Lord; as time goes by, I'm able to let go of the possessions more and more. I'm able to focus on You and to be satisfied with this new life and Your precious gift. Remind me of the joy in simply trusting You!

He chooses our inheritance for us,
the glory of Jacob whom He loves. Selah.
--Psalm 47:4

Day 181

4/23/16

The thing about being married is that you have a built-in helper, well hopefully, anyway. When you are without your spouse—it's very humbling because you have to ask people to help you—a lot. And that is hard!!

Thank You, Lord; I know you have a plan for all of my needs! Thank You--I get to lean on You for everything, always and forever!

When I am afraid,

I will put my trust in Thee.

--Psalm 56:3

Day 182

9/21/16

Yesterday, I got the tiniest little glimpse of some joy—it came peeking out of my heart! Thank You, Lord! And with it came some excitement about things ahead...a craft show in the country, the Ladies Retreat and a short trip to set up a wedding cake. Anticipation, yay!

I guess I have felt so encumbered in the last several months, just feeling barely able to walk through the days. Thank You, Lord, for lightening it up for me! And Thank You for the glimpse of joy in my heart...I am looking forward to more bits of joy, until my final joy, being with You in Glory!

And these things we write,

so that our joy may be made complete.

And this is the message we have heard from Him and announce to you,

that God is light,

and in Him there is no darkness at all.

--1 John 1:4-5

Day 183

6/16/16

I'm still wondering why!!

Rule #1   Don't try to figure it out…it could hurt your brain. God knows!

A good part of our days are spent trying to figure stuff out and trying to fit life's happenings into some form that makes sense to us. If only we can do that…everything will, at least, seem ok?! Until the next un-understandable thing happens.

But God says…"Give it up; you were not meant to understand this. Instead, rest. I am able to guide you through, even when nothing makes sense! I know."

Thank You, Lord; I can count on You. You will carry this for me. And You will always carry me!

O Lord, my heart is not proud,

or my eyes haughty;

nor do I involve myself in great matters,

or in things too difficult for me.

—-Psalm 131:1

Day 184

3/21/16

With court, finally, possibly looming ahead--I'm spending way too much time trying to keep my thoughts from dwelling there. Oh, Dear Lord, please protect my thoughts. Just remind me of all the truth You have shown me over and over this last year.

Thank You, Lord, for this crazy adventure. This year (and more) that I never wanted to go through--looks as if it's almost over. Thank You, that You are indeed more powerful than anyone and anything.

Rule #8   God, indeed, is more powerful than everyone or everything. God is!

I pray that the eyes of your heart may be enlightened,

so that you may know what is the hope of His calling,

what are the riches of the glory of His inheritance in the saints,

and what is the surpassing greatness of His power toward us who believe.

These are in accordance with the working of the strength of His might

which He brought about in Christ,

when He raised Him from the dead,

and seated Him at His right hand in the heavenly places,

far above all rule and authority and power and dominion,

and every name that is named,

not only in this age, but also in the one to come.

And He put all things in subjection under His feet,

and gave Him as head over all things to the church,

which is His body,

the fullness of Him who fills all in all.

--Ephesians 1:18-23

Day 185

8/12/15

This week I found out that "he" filed a Victim Protection Order against me. This man to whom I committed my life, loved and care for... "he" cheated, lied, attacked, betrayed me, and continues to do so. This one who still says in notes to me—"I love you, I miss you, I want you to come home" while "he" is doing despicable things to me.

May I stop listening to "him" now??

From my distress I called upon the Lord;

the Lord answered me and set me in a large place.

The Lord is for me; I will not fear;

what can man do to me?

-–Psalm 118:5-6

Rule #3   No one gets to say who I am but God. God says!

Day 186

8/27/15

There are so many verses about the lies--lying lips, falsehoods, the mouth, tongue, etc. That's really why I stepped out--to leave behind the lies and to walk in truth.

Rule #2   (Don't believe anything "he" says!) Don't dialogue with the devil. God is truth!

But here in the midst of "his" lies, I am exhausted. I'm feeling depressed, weary, I'm crying, tired and afraid.

Oh Lord, help me. Keep showing me the truth first! Thank You, Lord; my lips will praise You!

Because Thy lovingkindness is better than life,

my lips will praise Thee.

So I will bless Thee as long as I live.

I will lift up my hands in Thy name.

My soul is satisfied as with marrow and fatness,

and my mouth offers praises with joyful lips

...for the mouths of those who speak lies will be stopped!

--Psalm 63:3-5 and 11b

Day 187

7/4/15

Rule #4   God will show you what you need to see. God sees!

From the beginning, I thought I had the burden of proof! Things were happening, little mysteries—what was going on? So I resolved to figure it out—with a plan to determine what it was and fix it, of course!

One day, a friend said, "You don't have to follow 'him', to try to see what 'he's' doing—God will show you what you need to see!" My friend was right! I had become so entangled in the mess that I was taking responsibility for it. And I could not see what God was doing!

These days I'm practicing waiting for God to show me the truth and everything that may separate me from seeing Him clearly! It is difficult to break these old patterns of trying to control my world, but it's worth the peace that walking with the Lord brings!

No soldier in active service entangles himself in the affairs

of everyday life,

so that he may please the one who enlisted him as a soldier.

--2 Timothy 2:4

Day 188

8/17/16

Rule #6   Lay down the *why*. God understands.

I left my home 544 days ago. And today I read an article on the internet about the different types of affairs. My heart is breaking…in pain! And then I realized how quickly I was drawn in to the questions again, questions such as why, how, etc.

Oh Lord, You are so fully able to lead us through even that which we cannot understand. You love us more than we will ever fathom! Thank You, Lord, for being my answer! Thank You for walking in this with me! And once again, I release to You the *why*. I give the wondering up to You; You understand! And You have the power to transform the *why*—into Thankfulness!

Let me hear Thy lovingkindness in the morning;

for I trust in Thee;

teach me the way in which I should walk,

for to Thee I lift up my soul.

--Psalm 143:8

Day 189

8/2/16

Maybe I'm ready to write the dreaded goodbye letter?! This thought reminds me of that scene in the movie, "Hello Dolly," where Streisand sings: "Goodbye-goodbye"…and she keeps singing it even though Matthau keeps trying to shut her up! Hysterical!!

Anyhow, this isn't the movies—maybe a letter is just the thing? I could say all the stuff I never got to say, such as "you stink, you're mean, you, you, you…" Oops--maybe I've gotten off track a little!

It's a bit of a jumble in my mind now—what would I even say. Nothing I say can change the last three years. I cannot will "him" to change what "he" did—back to that again. Good grief!

Thank You, Lord; You are unchanging and perfect in all Your ways! I cannot go down again into the swirl of thinking about "him" and all that's happened. I must look at You instead. Dear Lord—keep my eyes on You today; it's my safe place!

Blessed be the Lord, who daily bears our burden,

the God who is our salvation.

God is to us a God of deliverances;

and to God the Lord belong escapes from death.

--Psalm 68:19-20

Day 190

8/22/16

Oh Lord, there is no way to describe Your glory; You are so magnificent!

I have been hoping to talk about You with a certain person and today I got to really share about Your wonderful care and provisions. Thank You, Lord, for opportunities like this.

I know that when You are in our everyday conversations, it's really originating from our every moment walk with You! Thank You, Lord; You are awesome!

And they were all amazed at the greatness of God.

--Luke 9:43a

Day 191

7/15/15

Today I threw away an old purse. It wasn't vintage; mind you, that would be a problem as I love those vintage purses! This may have no meaning to you, but to me it's significant! You see, I was carrying that purse when I left home.

So I was going through some things and found it—worn out thing! I cleaned a few bits out of it, including our checkbook from a now closed account. I'm saying goodbye! And it's okay. I imagine I'll say goodbye lots more times, until this part I'm going through gets smaller and smaller!

But as these hard things are getter smaller, God, Thank You, Lord—you remain the same. You are steadfast, reliable, and meeting my needs one by one, every day. Thank You, Lord!

Praise the Lord!

Oh give thanks to the Lord,

for He is good;

for His lovingkindness is everlasting.

--Psalm 106:1

Day 192

5/13/15

"What if" … I think those two words put together are satan's motto. To me, they are sledge hammers, beating me down! I have to turn my back on those words because it smacks of: "I am smart enough to figure this out!" The fact is I'm not!

Praise You, God; You are wisdom. You have a plan for my life; You won't ever sleep on the job. You are paying attention. You are near and ready to guide me through anything in front of me today, even this moment. Thank You, Lord, for Your presence in my life!

"Because of the devastation of the afflicted,

because of the groaning of the needy,

now I will arise," says the Lord;

"I will set him in the safety for which he longs."

--Psalm 12:5

Day 193

9/1/15

This is the most tired and unfocused I've ever been in my life. It seems that every little thing just takes my strength away.

Thank You, Lord; I am having to totally depend on You for my strength. Help me do whatever You put in front of me. Thank You for these feelings of being out of control, unfocused, and confused. I know I can trust You to show me the way. Every day of my life You will carry me!

Search me, O God, and know my heart;

try me and know my anxious thoughts;

and see if there be any hurtful way in me,

and lead me in the everlasting way.

--Psalm 139:23-24

Day 194

3/31/16

Dear Sister, it is going to get better! I can say this because I have lived it! It may be that all you can do right now is cry. Cry out to the Lord; He is with you! Or maybe all you want to do is scream--scream to the Lord; He is with you!

Thank You, Lord; You love us. You chose us on purpose. You saved us to be with You forever.

Rule #8   God, indeed, is more powerful than everyone and everything. God is!

Bow Thy heavens, O Lord, and come down;

touch the mountains, that they may smoke.

Flash forth lightning and scatter them.

Send out Thy arrows and confuse them.

Stretch forth Thy hand from on high;

rescue me and deliver me out of great waters,

out of the hands of aliens.

Whose mouths speak deceit,

And whose right hand is a right hand of falsehood.

I will sing a new song to Thee, O God;

upon a harp of ten strings I will sing praises to Thee.

--Psalm 144:5-9a

Day 195

7/20/16

What is it about pain…it either immobilizes us, or drives us? But one thing is for sure—it gets our focus off of God and onto ourselves. If we are drawn away from looking to the Lord in our pain, it can grow and overwhelm!

But if we can take the pain to the feet of Christ—the one who truly understands and wholly bore our pain on the Cross, we'll find perfect peace there. The pain may still be present but in the midst of it, we are free to trust the Lord's care for us.

But I am afflicted and in pain;

may Your salvation, O God,

set me securely on high.

--Psalm 69:29

Day 196

9/2/16

I'm getting a sense of the orchestration again. That's the reason that God is allowing so much time to pass, while "he" is in contempt… because I need more time.

I need more time to come to terms with how I really think about all of this. I know that I don't want to carry around any bitterness or hatred in my heart. I feel that God is still bringing it to the surface.

Thank You, Lord, for time to see You work in me in these areas! Please keep working here until there is no hurtful way left!

Rule #5   God's time is perfect. God endures!

Every man's way is right in his own eyes,

but the Lord weighs the hearts.

To do righteousness and justice.

is desired by the Lord rather than sacrifice.

--Proverbs 21:2

Day 197

6/28/15

When I think about all the lies I never wanted to believe, I still wonder and condemn myself sometimes! It makes my heart hurt to think about the years of wondering and deception. Just how stupid am I?!

Thank You, Lord; I am not stupid at all. And when I see where I am today, not having to worry when "he's" coming home and if our marriage is over, I am truly thankful!! Thank You, Lord; You answered those questions. You've guided me each step. You shielded me from harm, You kept me and You loved me! Thank You, Lord. I'm counting on You to use those days to redeem them!

The Lord is my light and my salvation;

whom shall I fear?

The Lord is the defense of my life;

whom shall I dread?

--Psalm 27:1

Day 198

8/12/16

It has been a difficult thing--knowing when to speak and when to keep silent. I have mostly thought—I don't want to speak to "him." And, of course, when I have spoken, arguments were the only result.

So finally—we are at a standstill. I cannot get my things or my share; "he" will not do anything. We are silent.

This, by far, feels worse than anything that has come before! Oh, Lord, please speak to me! What do You want me to do. What should I say?? What is my part? What are You doing here?

Incline your ear and hear the words of the wise,

and apply your mind to my knowledge;

for it will be pleasant if you keep them within you,

that they may be ready on your lips.

So that your trust may be in the Lord.

I have taught today, even you.

Have I not written to you excellent things of counsels and knowledge.

to make you know the certainty of the words of truth

that you may correctly answer to him who sent you?

--Proverbs 22:17-21

Day 199

9/1/16

It is so difficult to put your hand in God's hands and walk with Him into the valleys. And it is difficult to have no idea when you might see the answer to your question…"Will I see justice?" Really, it's impossible!

Though I know my former loved one cannot do a thing to pay for "his" choices, which ruined our lives, I still want my share of what we built together. But I am powerless to get it! Holding God's hands in this, and waiting, is terribly awful! It bumps up against the question, "Will I trust You, Lord?"

Thank You, Lord, for another day to trust You!

And He said,

"I am God, the God of your father;

do not be afraid to go down to Egypt,

for I will make you a great nation there.

I will go down with you to Egypt,

and I will also surely bring you up again…"

--Genesis 46:3-4

Day 200

9/815

Today might be the first time that I've been able to earnestly say to the Lord: "Thank You for allowing this to happen to me!" It all still seems so strange; as if I'm in an alternate life, one that's adjacent to where I was living!

Thank You, Lord. I know You are with me. Thank You for loving me so much that You will allow such pain in order for me to know You more. I want to know You more; I want to know You more; the greatest thing in all my life is knowing You!

Thou hast taken account of my wandering,

put my tears in Thy bottle;

are they not in Thy book?

Then my enemies will turn back in the day when I call;

this I know, that God is for me.

--Psalm 56:8-9

Day 201

8/28/16

Even knowing that the one who tore apart my life cannot pay for what "he" has done--and knowing that Jesus paid for all of our sins...I still have a longing in my heart for "him" to pay. And I want "him" to be stopped from ever saying "I love you" to me again.

At this point, I think it's more about the control and manipulation. I don't want to feel that I'm being controlled by "his" actions and words anymore! I want to be free of it!

Thank You, Lord, for this inner struggle which brings me right to you. I'm face to face with Your patient lovingkindness. You will make all of this for my highest and best good in Your time and for Your glory!

> *For Christ also died for sins once for all,*
>
> *the just for the unjust,*
>
> *in order that He might bring us to God,*
>
> *having been put to death in the flesh,*
>
> *but made alive in the spirit;*
>
> *--1 Peter 3:18*

Rule #8 God, indeed, is more powerful that everyone and everything. God is!

Day 202

8/22/16

There is an underlying fear that has come upon me. Two days ago, on my birthday I got a card in the mail. It was from "him," addressed to my first name only and sent to my new address. I thought "he" didn't know where I was. That makes me feel uneasy, watched, and stalked!

After all that's happened in the last year and a half, I cannot trust anything "he" says or does! He wrote in the card about how much "he" misses and loves me and "he" sent $20. Wow!

Oh Lord, I know I can trust in You. In You there is no fear. You are safe; You are kind and You are truthful!

From my distress I called upon the Lord;

The Lord answered me and set me in a large place.

The Lord is for me; I will not fear:

What can man do to me?

It is better to take refuge in the Lord than to trust in man.

It is better to take refuge in the Lord than to trust in princes.

--Psalm 118:5-6 and 8-9

Day 203

9/17/16

I have been struggling with fear again. It's a little more noticeable since "he" found out my address and phone number.

I have lived with plenty of fear for years; it really escalated in the months before I left. I remember when I was really, really frightened at home, I would be very quiet. As if I thought, I'll be quiet and calm and maybe the anger will subside. Maybe I won't need to be afraid of "him" or the pain and loss I'm facing.

Thank You, Lord; I am safe in Your arms! No one can snatch me from Your arms! I have nothing to fear. I have no one to fear.

Rule #8   God, indeed, is more powerful than everyone and everything. God is!

You are protecting me. You are protecting Your children!

But know that the Lord has set apart the godly man for Himself;

The Lord hears when I call to Him.

Tremble, and do not sin;

Meditate in your heart upon your bed, and be still.

Offer the sacrifices of righteousness, and trust in the Lord.

--Psalm 4:3-4

Day 204

7/10/16

I tend to think in absolutes…all or nothing, never, always and forever! Good, right? God thinks a lot different from me! He bring so many subtle nuances to my life--it's amazing!

Because of this, sometimes when my brain thinks blah, blah, blah…I have to stop and wait for the Lord to bring the truth against my thinking. Sometimes it takes a few minutes or a day or two. But it is always worth the wait for Him to shine the light on my thinking. Often my thinking is just wrong—which can become sin!! And really…I'm just tired of rushing ahead without the Lord, and then having to apologize, yuck!!

Thank You, Lord; You are truth. You are smart! And my blah, blah never scares You; You just keep shining the light on it! And thanks for letting me laugh at myself when my life is just too funny for words!

Thus says the Lord, "Let not a wise man boast of his wisdom,

and let not the mighty man boast of his might,

let not the rich man boast of his riches,

but let him who boasts boast of this,

that he understands and knows Me,

that I am the Lord who exercises lovingkindness, justice,

and righteousness on earth; for I delight in these things."

--Jeremiah 9:23-24

Day 205

7/9/16

The end of the thirty days when "he" has to give me my share of the house and personal belongings is just four days away. I have waited a long, long time to be here!

I know in my mind that it is just stuff—but a part of me says, "Yes, You are worth it"! And that is the bottom line for me! Because when "he" chose someone else over me, "he" said, "You are worthless!"

For 506 days I've felt as though I'm trying to get "him" to take it back! I want "him" to stop saying I'm worthless! Oh, Dear Lord!

Rule #3   No one gets to say who I am but God. God says!

That is the truth. Lord, I'm taking it back myself. I'm not going to walk in "his" truth anymore. I'm going to walk with You! I'm going to trust You, listen to You and believe You!

An excellent wife, who can find?

For her worth is far above jewels.

--Proverbs 31:10

Day 206

11/13/15

Just heard last night that my sweet friend with small children has cancer. I am heartbroken for her! She has already endured so many hardships in life! But I was able to say that God is enough for you. That's because I truly know He is!

Thank You, Lord, for this building block in my life—knowing Your faithfulness! I know You are faithful because I have lived in it with You.

In their affliction He was afflicted.

And the angel of His presence saved them;

in His love and in His mercy He redeemed them;

and He lifted them and carried them all the days of old.

--Isaiah 63:9

Day 207

7/30/16

I believe love is a commitment. But stuff happens when you make that commitment and live it out. You form attachments and have emotions related to your spouse and to your life together.

When the covenant is broken by "him," where does that leave you? It is taking a while to unravel our lives--past, present and future. The sheer weight of emotion is huge! Thank You, Lord; You will never leave me!

"For I am convinced that neither death, nor life, nor angels,

nor principalities, nor things present, nor things to come, nor powers,

not height, nor depth, nor any other created thing,

shall be able to separate us from the love of God,

which is in Christ Jesus our Lord!"

--Romans 8:38-39

Day 208

9/5/15

It is so scary thinking about going before the judge. I keep rehearsing what answers I might give! You see, the person I love and committed my life to in marriage has said to the authorities that "he" is afraid of me! This is another layer of "his" deception! "He" has told them that "he" is a victim! It's so weird—how this can all get turned around!

Rule #1 *Girl,* **Don't try to figure it out…it could hurt your brain. God knows!**

Although I'm not hiding, I am scared that they will find me. I'm just going forward and seeking God's leadership in my life. And are they even looking for me to serve the legal documents?

The Lord has already told me what to say. Thank You, Lord! And when I go before the judge, I know You will be protecting and guiding me with Your presence.

But when they deliver you up,

do not become anxious about how or what you will speak;

for it shall be given you in that hour what you are to speak.

For it is not you who speak,

but it is the Spirit of your Father who speaks in you.

--Matthew 10:19-20

Wrap up: As it turned out the Victim Protection Order was never served on me. It was eventually dismissed as having no standing. Thank You, Lord, for Your protection on my life, again!

Day 209

10/9/15

Two years ago on our anniversary weekend away, something was already happening. He was texting with someone and it came to me. There was a secret relationship.

Dear Lord, please meet me here. I am under attack. I am frightened and so sad. Please show me the way!

If I should say, "My foot has slipped,"

Thy lovingkindness, O Lord, will hold me up.

When my anxious thoughts multiply within,

Thy consolations delight my soul.

--Psalm 94:18-19

Day 210

6/30/15

I'm still fighting this sense of dread! I'll be going along during my day, and then I remember that my husband left me. Thank You, Lord; You would never condemn me for this. You love me. I belong to You. Please keep reminding me of Your presence when those thoughts come to mind.

O Taste and see that the Lord is good;

How blessed is the man who takes refuge in Him!

--Psalm 34:8

Day 211

9/13/16

Today is the magical day--the end of the 30 days--the day "he" must give me my share or be in contempt of court. So far the threat of contempt in this situation has made no difference whatsoever.

Oh Lord, please make a difference. Please make "him" pay. I do not want to go on forever with things left like this! I hate the limbo!!

Thank You, Lord; You are building something here and I cannot understand it!

Rule #1   Don't try to figure it out…it could hurt your brain. God knows!

You are watching the entire situation and are intimately acquainted with my entire life! Please give me strength for today! Help me focus on You, Praise You and wait for You! I love You Lord—You are beautiful and full of glory!

For every house is built by someone,

but the builder of all things is God.

--Hebrews 3:4

Day 212

6/17/16

How do you stop loving someone? Even now, I have no idea. Thank You, Lord; this is all Yours to work out as You please.

I do believe God gave me a love for "him." I'm not talking about feelings, but a willingness to care for, give myself to, and commit to continue in relationship with "him." And since He gave that to me, I am trusting Him to take it away and to redirect my heart. Oh Lord, help me; this is difficult!

The Lord will accomplish what concerns me;

Thy lovingkindness, O Lord, is everlasting;

Do not forsake the works of Thy hands.

--Psalm 138:8

Day 213

8/23/15

In this world there is no guaranteed happiness, success or freedom. We may go along in life being perfectly nice, kind, and faithful, but that doesn't we will necessarily get it back! I suppose I have lived while making those things my aim. And having everyone like me has often been my goal as well. But that is exhausting!

Thank You, Lord; it is impossible to live in this world in peace and harmony without You. I get it; I'm getting it! You are peace and rest and love. That is who You are. Thank You, Lord; for showing me that I've been worshipping the things, not You. Please keep reminding me to bring my idols to You when they surface. I love You, Lord.

> *And we know that the Son of God has come,*
>
> *and has given us understanding,*
>
> *in order that we might know Him who is true,*
>
> *and we are in Him who is true, in His Son Jesus Christ.*
>
> *This is the true God and eternal life.*
>
> *Little children, guard yourself from idols.*
>
> *--1 John 5:20-21*

Rule #2   Don't dialogue with the devil. God is truth!

Day 214

9/5/15

I'm feeling as if I want to stop talking about all of this very soon. I'm tired of going over it…over and over. It's like being on a horrible carnival ride. You're trapped; you can't get off and you have to endure the torture and fear of it! Then when you finally do get off. (That's five minutes of your life you'll never get back) you can't stop talking about how bad it was and you keep reliving it in your mind.

Wow, that's exactly how this feels, where I am—only my horrible ride seems to never end! How I want to shake the dust off my feet!

Thank You, Lord; Your love is so powerful that You will allow all kinds of things in Your babies' lives so we will know You more fully! You allow it; and You walk with us through each one!

He will cover you with His pinions,

and under His wings you may seek refuge;

His faithfulness is a shield and bulwark.

--Psalm 91:4

Day 215

6/28/15

When friends and family begin to sense that you are doing better, they may stop checking on you. Their lives get busy and here you are…still dealing, feeling alone, wondering where you're headed, and what to do??? It's just a reminder that grief has no time limit. It's not necessarily over when we think it should be finished!

Thank You Lord; You are always with me. You never miss a thing! Thank You for dear friends and family who hold us up! Remind me they are a gift that You have given me!

Let the peace of Christ rule in your hearts,

to which indeed you were called in one body;

and be thankful.

--Colossians 3:15

Day 216

7/24/15

How sweet is this, Lord; I'm just realizing that You have shown me the quick truth before You showed me the lie! For months I have struggled with things "he" has said and whether or not to believe them! Many were just outright lies!

Then as I practiced trusting You and asking You to show me what to do, You began to show me the quick truth in each situation. Now it seems You have shown me the truth and then revealed the lie I was believing.

Thank You, Lord; You have brought me full circle into Your loving arms. I love You, Lord and I praise You; You are magnificent and beautiful to me!

Rule #4   God will show you what you need to see. God sees!

You, O Lord, will not withhold Your compassion from me;

Your lovingkindness and Your truth will continually preserve me.

--Psalm 40:11

Day 217

7/2/15

I crunched my car a little today and I cried. Of course, that many tears weren't warranted; after all I am a grown woman! But I cried. Maybe it was because now it looks bad--though it is still drivable. It just makes me sad and a little embarrassed.

So I prayed! Thank You, Lord, for reminding me that You are taking care of me. Thank You; You will help me get it fixed so I can open the hood! Thank You, Lord; You love me even when I make mistakes. Please give me some perspective, Lord.

I do know that some of the tears were for what I've lost this year! When you go through trauma, tears have a way of coming, as they are piled on top of current circumstances. And there is no way of controlling when the tears may fall. My brother came by from out of town. He said, "I'm surprised you're not crying because you stubbed your toe." He's a smart guy, I think!

Perspective--please Lord--help me see this from Your perspective!

And the ransomed of the Lord will return

and come with joyful shouting to Zion,

with everlasting joy upon their heads,

they shall obtain joy and gladness,

and sorrow and sighing shall flee away.

--Isaiah 35:10

Day 218

7/30/15

I had thought deep in my heart that "he" would stop. That "he" would finally admit to the sin that broke our marriage. In fact, I can see now that I've been waiting for that to happen all this time. But much time has passed and I have grown in the Lord--really been changed. His truth has set me free.

And "he" has not changed at all. "He" is still trying to shame and manipulate me with words and actions. "He" is still walking in the darkness of lies and deceit.

Thank You, Lord; You have come to shine the light on this world!

O send out Thy light and Thy truth, let them lead me;

Let them bring me to Thy Holy hill, and to Thy dwelling places.

Then I will go to the altar of God, to God my exceeding joy;

and upon the lyre I shall praise Thee,

O God, my God.

--Psalm 43:3-4

Day 219

8/26/15

Today I paid a bill I did not owe! It was "his" electric bill for our house, which I've been locked out of for months. Lord, I am mad! I feel angry!

Thank You, Lord; You provided the extra funds to pay the bill this week through an anonymous gift. Thank You, Lord, that You are watching; You are the judge and You see!

"When I select an appointed time,
it is I who judge with equity."
--Psalm 75:2

Wrap up: The judge ruled a year later that "he" should pay this bill and I did receive reimbursement!

Day 220

9/26/15

Oh, Dear Lord, I know You are with me! The first day of fall was this week. The mornings seem gloomier when I wake up. But I love the fall with its trees turning their leaves and the cool breezes.

I can look out my front window and see trees. I'm thankful for that. But I miss my old house and those tall old trees. The yards were filled with leaves and we would just leave them on the ground until spring.

Changing season, please give me a reason to rejoice over my new place. I have hardwood floors, room for my work, my own driveway and flowerpots on my porch. I have food to eat and work to do, plus my mother's and grandmother's things around me. The big blue trash can is right outside the kitchen door, so I don't have to carry things too far.

Thank You, Lord; You are with me! And I can be thankful just for that! And You have met so many of my needs--even some I didn't realize I had!

How precious also are Thy thoughts to me, O God!

How vast is the sum of them.

If I should count them, they would outnumber the sand.

When I awake, I am still with Thee.

--Psalm 139:17-18

Day 221

10/11/15

There is nothing like a day away to remind you that it's good to be home! I have had a hard time accepting that this is my home now. Don't get me wrong; I'm glad to be away from the turmoil, but I liked my house and the neighborhood. I'm in a different place now!

Thank You, Lord; I can be grateful for Your provision. Your gifts are good. I can trust You to work out my life and my needs. Thank You, Lord, for meeting my needs!

It is good to give thanks to the Lord,

and to sing praises to Thy name, O Most High;

to declare Thy lovingkindness in the morning,

and Thy faithfulness by night.

--Psalm 92:1-2

Day 222

10/29/15

Today, I'm thankful for a clock radio. I was using my old phone for an alarm clock, but it was taken in the burglary of my home. And my new phone alarm isn't very loud. So, when you go to buy an alarm clock…it might come with a radio!

It is so wonderful to be able to hear some Christian music when I'm getting ready in the morning, and just before I sleep!

Thank You, Lord, for meeting my needs and showing me the desires of my heart, and for being with me in every detail!

Trust in the Lord, and do good;

Dwell in the land and cultivate faithfulness.

Delight yourself in the Lord;

and He will give you the desires of your heart.

Commit your way to the Lord, trust also in Him and He will do it.

--Psalm 37:3-5

Day 223

11/15/15

The physical exhaustion and stress are plaguing me again! O, Dear Lord, keep my mind turned to You! Please help me rest in You!

The Lord is your keeper;

The Lord is your shade on Your right hand.

The sun will not smite you by day,

Nor the moon by night. The Lord will protect you from evil;

He will keep your soul

The Lord will guard your going out

and your coming in from this time forth and forever.

--Psalm 121:5-8

Day 224

2/28/16

Finally, I have a little peace! Thank You, Lord; for the breather from the bad stuff! Thank You, Lord, for spring flowers and the sunshine!

Blessed be the Lord, my rock,

who trains my hands for war, and my fingers for battle;

my lovingkindness and my fortress, my stronghold and my deliverer;

my shield and He in whom I take refuge;

who subdues my people under me.

O Lord, what is man, that Thou dost think of him?

Man is a mere breath; his days are like a passing shadow.

–Psalm 144:1-4

I will sing a new song to Thee, O God;

upon a harp of ten strings, I will sing praises to Thee.

--Psalm 144:9

Day 225

3/25/16

Today I'm faced with the same idea as every day of the past year. Am I going to trust the Lord? Am I going to walk with Him in the scariest of times, even when I feel so scared I get paralyzed?

For today, for this moment—I will choose Him!

Thank You, Lord, for the precious gift of choosing. Thank You for calling to me from the Cross and for loving me before I knew You!

Therefore, brethren,

be all the more diligent to make certain about His calling

and choosing you;

for as long as you practice these things,

you will never stumble;

for in this way the entrance into the eternal kingdom

of our Lord and Savior Jesus Christ

will be abundantly supplied to you.

--Peter 1:10-11

Day 226

8/26/15

After much tossing and turning, this morning I woke up with a sad countenance. This is not surprising--"he" has done another really cruel thing to me! And I can't really form thoughts, so I just say, "Jesus, Jesus, Jesus." I am confident that the Lord heard my heart cry!

So while going about my day, a lady I swim with begins sharing with me. She's talking about having peace. She also talked about being who God made you and walking in that! And about trusting the Lord through good and bad. Now I am able to say, "That's right, God is working through the pain!"

Thank You, Lord; You use the pain to grow us up and to continue us on in our dependence on You. Thank You, Lord, for using Your child to minister to me!

Let us hold fast the confession of our hope without wavering,

for He who promised is faithful

and let us consider how to stimulate one another to love and good deeds,

not forsaking our own assembling together, as is the habit of some,

but encouraging one another,

and all the more, as you see the day drawing near.

--Hebrews 10:23-25

Day 227

7/8/15

A slow, gradual sense that I'm moving forward is happening. I must be moving forward; it feels like it and looks like it...! Each day I'm able to get a little more organized, and to take steps to put my life back together. I am spending less time thinking of myself as a victim.

Dear Lord! Thank You so much for each of these steps! If I had not turned to You, I would be lost! Thank You, Lord, for sustaining me and showing me which direction to go. Thank You for holding me here--wherever here is! Thank You for each day when there's a tiny flower of hope growing a little bigger in my heart!

Shot joyfully to God, all the earth;

sing the glory of His name;

make His praise glorious.

Say to God, "How awesome are Thy works!'

--Psalm 66:1-3

Day 228

7/3/15

In addition to "Why did "he" do that," I've spent plenty of time asking, "Why did I let this happen? How could I be so foolish as to not see this coming?" Those questions are all about bringing shame to myself for not being perfect. Did I really expect to be perfect?

Thank You, Lord; I am not perfect! Thank You for being perfect, wise, and capable. You did actually see all of this and You are working. You are longsuffering in the middle of us flailing about in our world! You are not surprised!

There is therefore now no condemnation

for those who are in Christ Jesus.

--Romans 8:1

Day 229

9/3/15

I think the most difficult thing in all of this might be the "spin out." It's the battle in my mind! What do I do? Am I fighting for me, or for justice? Am I fighting for what God wants? Or all of it might be the same thing--I'm just not certain sometimes!

Thank You, Lord; You have given me a new mind! And You are renewing my mind day after day. Oh Dear Lord, grant me grace to walk with You even when the thoughts are swirling around in my head!

Therefore, gird your minds for action;

keep sober in spirit,

fix your hope completely on the grace to be brought to you

at the revelation of Jesus Christ.

--1 Peter 1:13

Day 230

7/1/15

Today the Lord comforted my heart!

For our heart rejoices in Him,

because we trust in His Holy name.

--Psalm 33:21

I would be lying if I said I haven't given some thought to hurting the one who hurt me so deeply! I have thought things, prayed about them and given them over to God. It's because I do trust the Lord that I know it all rests with Him. Thank You, Lord; You know!

Today, as I was thinking about the situation, the Lord brought to mind that "he" lost "his" wife. The Lord said to me, "Even if that is all that ever happens to "him," that is huge!" I loved "him", cared for "him". I am precious and beautiful… and "he" lost me! Thank You, Lord, for showing me that You are already at work taking care of vengeance and retribution!

The Lord can do a great deal with our thoughts about ourselves when we listen. He is the very foundation of us, who we are, what we think of ourselves and how we see others. And by the way, no one has more power than God to give us our worth. The person in your life who has defined you in the wrong way--is wrong!

Rule #3   No one gets to say who I am but God. God says!

Day 231

8/30/15

Oh, Dear Lord, please help me. I feel that I'm in the deepest ditch ever. I get a glimpse of Your peace every now and then, but then--the torment overtakes me. I am afraid of the future. I'm afraid that "he" will win with the lies. That I'm being punished for leaving behind "his" adultery. Oh Dear Lord, I know the victory is Yours. Please help me see!

Rule #4   God will show you what you need to see. God sees!

And the nations will see your righteousness, and all the kings your glory.

And you will be called by a new name,

which the mouth of the Lord will designate.

You will also be crown of beauty in the hand of the Lord,

and a royal diadem in the hand of your God.

It will no longer be said to you, "Forsaken,"

nor to your land will it any longer be said, "Desolate";

but you will be called, "My delight is in her,"

--Isaiah 62:2-4a

Day 232

9/25/15

I thought that knowing "he" cheated was hard, then having "him" leave our life and having to explain it to friends, *that* was hard. When "he" pretended it didn't happen, that was so difficult. Now letting go of all the things that I had to leave in the house, all the things that I will probably never see again, this is the new hard thing!!

I might get some comfort knowing that "he'll" have to clear out all of it to put the house on the market; no, it's still really kind of unbearable!

Thank You, Lord, I don't ever want these things to cause me to be separated from You! I don't want to have to carry them along with me. They aren't more important than YOU! Nothing is! Lord, keep me close, open my heart, and help me release them!

Let your way of life be free from the love of money (things),

being content with what you have;

for He Himself has said, "I will never desert you,

nor will I ever forsake you,"

so that we confidently say,

"The Lord is my helper, I will not be afraid. What shall man do to me?"

--Hebrews 13:5-6

Day 233

9/27/15

I'm not sure who I am now. After almost eighteen years of being married to someone, your identity can get a little blurred! I'm making an effort to ask the Lord about the many little decisions I'm facing. Instead of waltzing ahead trying to recapture all I've lost, I want to allow Him to make me new!

Thank You, Lord; it's a new day--a new day to praise You. It's a new day to walk with You and a new day to trust You!

...and put on the new self,

which in the likeness of God has been created

in righteousness and holiness of the truth.

--Ephesians 4:24

Day 234

7/14/15

No matter how I try, I cannot seem to escape all of the garbage left in the wake of this mess "he" has made of our lives. I still struggle with this almost every day.

Thank You, Lord; You have seen each of my days and You know each one. You are strong enough to hold me up out of the garbage! You are not surprised by anything and You want to train us up to give You all the glory. Lord, I know that I am already free of it! Thank You, Lord; please remind me to focus on You and not on all of these things that try to draw me away from You!

Thine eyes have seen my unformed substance;

and in Thy book they were all written,

the days that were ordained for me,

when as yet there was not one of them.

--Psalm 139:16

Day 235

You'll want to hurry things along.

Rule #5   God's time is perfect. God endures!

It seems perfectly fine to try to rush ahead and try to fix things in the hope of righting some of the chaos. Wait! The Lord has a special plan for you, His baby. He is working! You may not see it for a little while but when you do, You'll be praising the Lord! Thank You, Lord, for perfect timing.

But you will not go out in haste,

nor will you go as fugitives;

for the Lord will go before you,

and the God of Israel will be your rearguard.

-–Isaiah 52:12

Day 236

7/30/15

    I've been practicing meeting the Lord in the morning for a while. Now I'm noticing a longing for time with Him at the end of the day. I want some closure or a debriefing right before I sleep. I guess I'm making new routines.

    But since I'm still unpacking my household and finding a place for things, a study area is not to be had. What this really means is that my table is piled high with boxes, etc.!

    So I tried a little singing to the Lord. It seemed like a perfect way to offer a sacrifice of praise to the One who ordered my day! I know the Lord is so happy to hear the voices of His babies. Thank You, Lord, for hearts to know You and voices raised to praise Your Holy Name.

For Thou, O Lord, hast made me glad by what Thou has done.
I will sing for joy at the works of Thy hands.
--Psalm 92:4

Day 237

8/10/15

There is this feeling that I am alone and You have left me. I hate that feeling! It is not that things are going wrong, but You just seem far away. I know that this is the time to lean into You, to watch for Your presence all around me! But it's hard, Lord!

Thank You, Lord; whether I feel like it or not, You are with me. I cannot get away from You. You love me and are living in me.

Where can I go from Thy Spirit?
Or where can I flee from Thy presence?
If I ascend to heaven, Thou art there;
if I make my bed in Sheol, behold, Thou art there.
If I take the wings of the dawn,
if I dwell in the remotest part of the sea,
even there Thy hand will lead me,
and Thy right hand will lay hold of me.

--Psalm 139:7-10

Day 238

8/13/15

Every little moment I hear, "Poor thing, look what "he" took from you; "he" has everything. What are you going to do now?" These thoughts are bombarding me every day!!

Thank You, Lord; You have given me Your truth to fight this battle. I have You speaking it in my ear to remind me. Thank You, Lord, for putting me through this discipline. You are building Your truth into me.

My son, do not reject the discipline of the Lord,

or loathe His reproof,

for who the Lord loves He reproves,

even as a father corrects the son in whom He delights.

--Proverbs 3:11

Rule #2   Don't dialogue with the devil. God is truth!

Day 239

8/24/15

Rule #7   God's arm is long enough to walk with me every step. God loves!

Is God enough? That's what I'm having trouble with today; I know He has proven Himself faithful over and over. I know His word says that He is faithful! BUT…

God is big enough. He has met so many needs today I can hardly believe it! Thank You, Lord, for answering my questions in a sweet and awesome way!

O my strength, I will sing praises to Thee;

For God is my stronghold,

the God who shows me lovingkindness.

--Psalm 59:17

Day 240

9/10/15

Rule #5 God's time is perfect. God endures!

There is nothing like waiting on the Lord! On one hand, there is a restlessness and many questions: "What are You doing, Lord? When will this be over? Can I live through this?" "Are You even working?"

On the other hand, there is the pure joy of it. "I cannot wait to see what God is going to do next." "Did you see that?" And there is peace in my heart as I practice resting in Him, waiting on Him, and growing while He brings about my life.

Yesterday I saw a tiny but huge detail in my life work out for good! I was blindsided by evil done by my spouse. The evil was immediately followed by God's sweet aroma. The Lord worked it out for good in a miraculous way. It was in a way that no human being could have created. And it was amazing!

Thank You, Lord; You have such perfect timing! You bring together events from two different time frames and use them to give to Your babies just what they need!

Wait for the Lord; be strong,

and let your heart take courage;

Yes, wait for the Lord.

--Psalm 27:14

Day 241

10/11/15

It is one week until our anniversary and it's has been heavy on my mind! Last year we went to a craft show where "he" bought me a bracelet. I found out later that "he" bought one for her too! Two years ago there was a text—obviously meant for "her" but "he" sent it to me instead.

Oh Lord, I can spend the next week rehearsing all of these hurtful things. Or I can choose to lay each of them down as You bring them to mind. I think that's what I'll do! Because I don't want to lose another moment to anger and bitterness! Especially not when I can spend those moments rejoicing in all You have done in my life!

Thank You, Lord! You are showing me the light. Please give me extra strong light this week!

Jesus therefore said to them,

"For a little while longer the light is among you.

Walk while you have the light,

that darkness may not overtake you;

he who walks in the darkness does not know where he goes."

--John 12:35

Day 242

7/15/17

I had a really big cry last night about what I've lost and how it feels like God just left me here. Thank You, Lord; today I can understand how You were showing me some lies that I've been believing about You!

1) You will leave me. Total lie! You will never leave me or forsake me!
2) You have no power in this situation. Lie! Power and dominion belong to You; You are sovereign!
3) I will be here forever at "his" mercy, and stuck in this mess that "he" has made! Lie! You are faithful; Your mercies endure forever. Vengeance is Yours, Lord!

Thank You, Lord, for the truth!

Rule #2   Don't dialogue with the devil. God is truth!

For the kingdom of God

does not consist in words but in power.

--1 Corinthians 4:20

Day 243

7/25/15

How can a flat tire be a curse to one person and a joy to another? Well, today I had a flat tire and I was stuck on the frontage road. It was very hot but I had water and a snack. Someone from church came and rescued my perishable groceries. I waited for the tow truck. The first one drove by and reported to his dispatcher that he could not change my tire because of where I was parked. I didn't know this until I'd been there for an hour. So my Roadside Assistance sent another truck. This time the driver blocked my car from oncoming traffic, got me into the air conditioned cab and changed my tire. I could have spent that whole time griping, but I prayed instead. In the end, I was well taken care of by the Lord.

And I guess I could spend these tough days griping. I could just sit in this mess. But is it possible that losing everything could be a joy to me?? I know now that it is completely true. While I'm getting divorced I can find joy in this place. I can see God working, even when things go wrong. I would never recommend this to anyone but because of the love of God, I'm able to be here and still be all right!

Thank You, Lord. I never wanted to go here; I tried not to go here. But God, You are bringing me through this. You love me and care for me. I give You all the glory, Lord, for showing me Your joy in the midst of great sorrow. Because of You I can face today and tomorrow with You!

God thunders with His voice wondrously,

doing great things which we cannot comprehend.

--Job 37:5

Day 244

9/20/15

I realize now that no amount of yelling will change a thing!

Rule #1   Don't try to figure it out…it could hurt your brain. God knows!

I woke up from two dreams about "him." In the first dream I was in our house (which I've been locked out of for months) and "he" was there. I was looking through the rooms and all of our things were gone. (Did I mention that "he's" been holding them hostage for months?) And there were lots of staging furniture and things everywhere. ("He" put the house on the market without consulting me on price or realtor). And I was yelling at "him!"

I've yelled at him a lot in the last three years. Sometimes until I was hoarse! But I have felt I had no voice. "He" just kept on walking down this marriage destroying path. And here we are!

Thank You, Lord; You hear me. You hear when I praise You and when my cry is filled with tears and anguish. Thank You, Lord; You care for me and You don't mock my pain. And though Your pain and suffering outweighed mine beyond comprehension, You still loved me! I love You, Lord!

Out of the depths I have cried to Thee, O Lord.

Lord, hear my voice!

Let Thine ears be attentive to the voice of my supplications.

--Psalm 130:1-2

Day 245

7/6/15

It doesn't take much to trigger memories, especially after eighteen years. There are a lot of memories. But I have trouble unpacking them and knowing what to do with them. At this point I really don't want to foster any happy thoughts about "him" or our life together! "He" has left, and I have been released by the Lord from the covenant I made. I need a fresh start.

Thank You, Lord; You completely understand everything! Please help me know what to do with these memories, feelings, and ponderings. And keep me putting one foot in front of the other!

I will lift up my eyes to the mountains;

from whence shall my help come?

My help comes from the Lord,

who made heaven and earth.

He will not allow my foot to slip;

He who keeps you will not slumber.

--Psalm 121:1-3

Day 246

9/20/15

In the second dream (see Day 244) I was in the garage and the kitchen of our house. My sister was there too. I must have brought her to my dream for moral support!

I was still yelling at "him" and "he" was just smiling at me. I find that very annoying! I seem to remember that "he" used to do that in the months before I left home. And "he" would say, "You just don't like being out of control." Wow, that's scary, sadistic behavior.

In the dream, as I was leaving, I started picking up the things that I wanted. Then all the drawers in the kitchen were empty! I remember thinking that I was disappointed because I was looking for my cake knife and server!

Thank You, Lord; I don't like being out of control. But I do like Your being in control of my life! You are just, Lord, and kind, and loving. I know I can count on You to want the highest and best for my life. You, Dear Lord, are trustworthy!

Those who trust in the Lord are as Mount Zion,

which cannot be moved, but abides forever.

--Psalm 125:1

Day 247

8/20/15

Yesterday was my birthday—it was a tough day. I was happy to spend the day with family and friends but thoughts of "him" kept creeping across my mind.

I found myself thinking about this past year and all the things "he" did to abandon and break our marriage. I guess I did this to remind myself that I am better off now. I went over and over the holidays last year and rehearsed the hurts. I realized "he" wasn't really with me during those times anyway!

Oh help me, Lord. I thank You, Lord—first, for making me and intricately forming me! Thank You, Lord, for celebrating me, Your creation. Second, Thank You that I am Yours, washed clean by the blood of Your Son! Thank You that Your Spirit lives in me, showing me Yourself each moment! And Thank You for being my husband; You are unchangeable, perfect, loving, and attentive!

For your husband is your Maker,

whose name is the Lord of host;

and your Redeemer is the Holy One of Israel,

who is called the God of all the earth.

--Isaiah 54:5

Day 248

7/9/15

This bond that God has created cannot be undone by us. The marriage covenant is a strong and lasting bond. Being bonded together with someone who has stepped away from the relationship is my struggle today. As hard as I try, I cannot un-bond what the Lord has put together.

Thank You, Lord, for showing me this.

Rule #4   God will show you what you need to see. God sees!

Thank You, Lord; my future is in You. You will teach me how to walk in it and You are re-creating my life alone with You!

Thou will make known to me the path of life;

in Thy presence is fullness of joy;

in Thy right hand there are pleasures forever.

--Psalm 16:11

Day 249

10/26/15

There is still so much anxiety every day. Oh Dear Lord, please envelope me in Your peace. Please help me see what to let go of so I can experience You more. Please keep me in Your perfect timing—even when I want to spin around in my plans.

Thank You, Lord; You have plans for me and I cannot accomplish them by anxiously looking around to know what to do next! Thank You, for in You, I can rest and watch Your life in me unfold!

Rule #5   God's time is perfect. God endures!

Therefore don't be anxious for tomorrow;

for tomorrow will care for itself.

Each day has enough trouble of its own.

--Matthew 6:34

Day 250

10/26/15

Tomorrow is a dear friend's wedding…the next day would have been our 18th anniversary.

Today—Oh Lord, please help me! I don't want to take away from her day—her lovely wedding. But I am in pain. How am I possibly going to make it through this wedding?

Thank You, Lord; there is no way for me to go to this event and not feel some of the sadness. But I know You will be there with me. Thank You; You will be speaking love in my ear. I can walk through tomorrow because of You, Lord!

But let all who take refuge in Thee be glad,

let them ever sing for joy;

And mayest Thou shelter them,

that those who love Thy name may exult in Thee.

For it is Thou who does bless the righteous man, O Lord,

Thou dost surround him with favor as with a shield.

--Psalm 5:11-12

Day 251

10/31/15

It's a sweet thing to have my cat with me! After months of her being locked in our house, she is here. She is a warm companion and a steady friend! She cuddles up on the cold nights and 'helps' me have some quiet time with the Lord.

Thank You, Lord, for this gift! If not for this precious friend, my house would be too quiet and empty. Thank You for giving me comfort in this small creature! You've given me something to care for—something to fill my empty arms. Thank You, Lord!

Enter His gates with thanksgiving, and His courts with praise.

Give thanks to Him, bless His name.

For the Lord is good; His lovingkindness is everlasting,

and His faithfulness to all generations.

--Psalm 100:4-5

Day 252

12/18/15

I never knew that while this was happening to me, it was also happening to a dear sister at church! This realization has made it twice as horrible! And I feel that it's brought me back to square one just a bit.

Help me, Lord, to refocus on You! Thank You, Lord, for walking me through this journey. Thank You for the opportunity to walk with my sister through her fight too.

I will remember the deeds of the Lord;

surely I will remember Your wonders of old.

I will meditate on all Your work and muse on Your deeds.

Your way, O God, is holy; what god is great like our God?

You are the God who works wonders;

You have made known Your strength among the peoples.

You have by Your power redeemed Your people,

the sons of Jacob and Joseph. Selah.

--Psalm 77:11-15

Day 253

4/12/16

When things are going well, I am tempted to rest a little. But I think that God is more in the front of my mind when I'm in the tough times. I'll be thinking: "What's next, Lord!" But my hope is that I have equal dependence in the good times and the bad.

Thank You, Lord; dependence on You is an everyday and every moment thing. You don't choose which times to be with Your babies. You are always here!

For this reason also, since the day we heard of it,

we have not ceased to pray for you

and to ask that you may be filled with the knowledge of His will

in all spiritual wisdom and understanding,

so that you may work in a manner worthy of the Lord,

to please Him in all respects,

bearing fruit in every good work and increasing in the knowledge of God;

strengthened with all power, according to His glorious might,

for the attaining of all steadfastness and patience,

joyously giving thanks to the Father,

who has qualified us to share in the inheritance of the saints in light.

--Colossians 1:9-12

Day 254

6/29/16

Three years ago I walked into a counseling room to meet a lady. I had no idea of the journey that God had planned for me and no idea who this gal was that was making a commitment to walk through it with me!

We saw lots of tears and fears along the way. Each of them was seen by God, too. She kept telling me: "Only God can change a life." When I wanted to give up week after week, she stood fast in the truth and told me who God is over and over! And she told me who I am--His precious baby!

Many times when I didn't do my homework, she still hung in there with me, because she could see God working. Thank You, Lord, for giving me someone to walk with on this super difficult path. You gave me a friend who keeps pointing out the ways to You.

Thank You, Lord, for Your gracious faithfulness! And thank You for this wonderful journey with You. I guess it is true that only God can change a life…any way He pleases!

For nothing will be impossible with God.

--Luke 1:37

Day 255

12/24/15

Today a friend has asked to have a copy of the 7 Rules to share with his friend. Initially I said, "No, I want to pray about it!" I thought sharing them might be bad since I am planning to publish the things the Lord is showing me.

As I prayed, I realized that sharing this work now and in the future is what God has put on my heart. So published in book form or handwritten in the worn, overflowing folder I have right now--this is what God has given me to share! Bless the Lord!

I will bless the Lord at all times;

His praise shall continually be in my mouth

My soul shall make boast in the Lord;

The humble shall hear it and rejoice.

O magnify the Lord with me.

And let us exult His name together.

--Psalm 34:1-3

Day 256

8/8/16

Rule #2 Don't dialogue with the devil. God is truth!

I still see self creeping in, even after all I've been through, after every step You've led me. I call her 'judgy' Susi. She so wants to rule me and she can really put me down! She whispers the following to my soul, "You are a failure." "What are you doing?" "You are stupid!" "You are worthless." Okay, sometimes she shouts! Yuck-- just spending a moment listening is so devastating!

Oh Dear Lord, Thank You for making the lies and the truth so clear to me. Keep me walking in Your truth!

These are the things you should do:

Speak the truth to one another;

Judge with truth and judgment for peace in your gates.

--Zechariah 8:16

Day 257

11/3/15

Even now I am still fighting the doubts and it's been 257 days since I left home! But God has been showing me that I have been fighting for our marriage every day.

Marriage, as God intended, would be full of love, commitment and fidelity. Even more than just 'not' cheating, we would be actually choosing the other one's highest and best good!

That is what I'm fighting for. When I stepped out by faith, I was asking God to do that in our marriage. When "he" made it clear that "he" was choosing someone else, I was still asking the Lord what to do. And the Lord answered. God said to my heart that "he" has broken the covenant that "he" made with you; I am now releasing you.

I thank You, Lord; You are as faithful today as You were 257 days ago! Thank You for seeing and knowing and loving me enough through all these difficult things and training me in my dependence on You!

O Give thanks to the Lord,

call upon His name;

make known His deeds among the peoples,

sing to Him, sing praises to Him;

speak of all His wonders.

Glory to His Holy name;

let the heart of those who seek the Lord be glad.

--Psalm 105:1-3

Day 258

11/5/15

Rule #1   Don't try to figure it out…it could hurt your brain. God knows.

I am amazed at how situations are so often not what they seem. It is amazing that when we are walking with Lord, we get an opportunity to wait for Him to work in the situation.

Yesterday I found out that the man I am still married to will not listen to "his" lawyer. "He" will not move forward. I am shocked--I hope I will always be shocked by selfishness, lies, and deceit! And I'm so interested to know what are You going to do with that, Lord!

Thank You, Lord; Your hand is on this and every other moment of our lives. You know what's happening! You are paying attention!

But Thou, O Lord, art a shield about me,

my glory, and the One who lifts my head.

I was crying to the Lord with my voice,

and He answered me from His holy mountain.

I lay down and slept; I awoke, for the Lord sustains me.

--Psalm 3:3-5

Day 259

4/1/16

Grief is without boundaries. Some days it is long and heavy and other days it's hardly thought of at all. The grief regarding infidelity, unfaithfulness, abandonment and deceit are nothing to be shrugged off! These are real causes for grief and they are beyond comprehension! And similar to losing a loved one, this grief has its own timeframe.

Thank You, Lord; You fully understand all of our grief and sorrow. You are able and willing walk this path with us! You hear our pain and hold us.

I am weary with sighing;

every night I make my bed swim,

I dissolve my couch with my tears.

My eye has wasted away with grief;

it has become old because of all my adversaries.

Depart from me, all you who do iniquity,

for the Lord has heard the voice of my weeping.

--Psalm 6:6-7

Day 260

6/27/16

I finally have some of my things, but I'm not certain it's worth it! I did function 16 months without these things. They feel heavy! Oh Lord, please help me.

There are a few things that I want to keep, but many are going in a yard sale. There is so much to decide; I'm so happy I didn't have to do this a year ago when I could barely see straight. It's even difficult after all this time. Oh Lord, please help me.

Thank You, Lord, for the things I did get and for the money that the yard sale will bring. Thank You for the little things I can use and enjoy--things that make me happy.

And he began reasoning to himself, saying,
"What shall I do, since I have no place to store my crops?"
And he said, "This is what I will do:
I will tear down my barns and build larger ones,
and there I will store all my grain and my goods.
And I will say to my soul,
"Soul, you have many goods laid up for many years to come;
take your ease, eat, drink and be merry."
But God said to him, 'You fool!
This very night your soul is required of you;
and now who will own what you have prepared?'
--Luke 12:17-20

Day 261

3/10/16

I keep thinking about court—what will I do and say. What will it be like to have to see "him" again? Will I get anything in the settlement?

And after court, when the divorce is final—I'll have to change my name on everything in my life because I just cannot bear the thought of carrying "his" name around anymore!

Oh, Dear Lord, please keep preparing me for that day. I know You are with me, waiting and watching, and caring!

> *He delivered me from my strong enemy,*
> *and from those who hated me,*
> *for they were too mighty for me.*
> *They confronted me in the day of my calamity,*
> *but the Lord was my stay.*
> *He brought me forth also into a broad place;*
> *He rescued me, because He delighted in me.*
> *--Psalm 18:17-19*

Day 262

2/23/16

It's February here in Oklahoma which means it's time for plants to start coming up, sending up buds and looking a little less like winter. I've been missing the Crocus flowers that I saw from my back windows for the last 15 years. They are these tiny little buttercups of flowers that show up amongst the snow and dry leaves. It was sheer joy to see them signaling spring.

The yards here have nothing--barely any grass--they look dry and sad! But yesterday as I was pulling out of my driveway, I glanced at my neighbor's yard and there was a gift from God. Two little yellow Crocus flowers had popped up in a sea of brown grass.

Thank You, Lord; You intricately design each part of Your world. You do this each day of our lives and each step of our journey with You!

Rule #7   God's arm is long enough to walk with me every step. God loves!

Therefore the Lord longs to be gracious to you,

and there He waits on High to have compassion on you.

For the Lord is a God of justice;

how blessed are all those who long for Him.

--Isaiah 30:18

Day 263

9/15/15

> *The wicked plots against the righteous,*
> *and gnashes at him with his teeth.*
> *The Lord laughs at him,*
> *for He sees his day is coming.*
>
> *--Psalm 37:12-13*

These verses are so perfect and delicious—I just had to share! You see, "he" cancelled my insurance ten weeks ago. This was in violation of the Temporary Order issued by the judge. This Temporary Order basically freezes our life together…so that neither party can change anything, like the mortgage, insurance matters, etc.!

As a result of the cancellation, a bill for my dental work came back to me unpaid! In the meantime, friends are seeing "him" out and about and "he" is showing off "his" new teeth.

A side note: Apparently my begging "him" for the last ten years to get dental work done has finally had an effect…!

Thank You, Lord; I can be confident that even the gnashing of teeth against me is of concern to You. You will take care of Your babies. You care for us in so many ways that we can't even understand. Thank You, Lord!

Day 264

6/25/15

Being so deeply hurt by the one you love might cause you to shy away from things you used to do together. Things like watching certain shows on TV or going to a restaurant you shared would be off limits. This would be fine, except—who wants to never have a Frito Chili Pie again? Or how about going to a craft mall or taking a small town road trip?

I guess the fun now is in spending these times with the Lord, letting Him direct my path and go there with me. Thank You, Lord, for longing to spend time with me! It's going to be okay. You will help me find my footing again!

"With weeping they will come,

and by supplication I will lead them;

I will make them walk by streams of waters,

on a straight path in which they will not stumble;

for I am a father to Israel, and Ephraim is My firstborn."

--Jeremiah 31:9

Day 265

8/3/15

 Once again my expectations overshot what You are doing, Lord! I ran ahead, not even realizing it. I've been so used to running ahead for so long! I looked at the situation, I assessed it, made a plan and did it. All the while I was second guessing and in the end, I'm still wondering if I did the right thing.

 Thank You, Lord; Your concern is about working in me even when I'm standing in the way. Thank You for showing me the truth about every little way I am still trying to run my life!

Therefore, since we have so great a cloud of witnesses surrounding us,

let us also lay aside every encumbrance,

and the sin which so easily entangles us,

and let us run with endurance the race that is set before us,

fixing our eyes on Jesus,

the author and perfecter of faith,

who for the joy set before Him,

endured the cross, despising the shame,

and has sat down at the right hand of the throne of God.

--Hebrews 12:1-2

Day 266

8/10/15

When I begin to feel that You are far away, it has been my habit to wrestle and wrestle to try to get back to You. Like so many other things in this life with You, I have it backwards!

Thank You, Lord; You will never leave me. There is nothing I can do to get You to leave me. Thank You, Lord; You are standing near me. You are waiting for me to put down my arms and to rest in You!

Behold, the eye of the Lord is on those who fear Him,

on those who hope for His lovingkindness,

To deliver their soul from death and keep them alive in famine.

--Psalm 33:18-19

Day 267

9/22/15

Again, I'm running ahead! I just want it to be over! I don't want to have to think about it anymore! I want my life back—I want to not be tied to "him!" I want to be untied and finally in my own life. But I am just jangling around in the mess!

Thank You, Lord; I can wait for You. Who am I kidding? I don't want to wait anymore! Thank You, Lord; You still love me, even when I'm wallowing in self-pity and mired in my own frustration!

And He will bring forth your righteousness as the light,

and your judgment as the noonday.

Rest in the Lord and wait patiently for Him;

fret not yourself because of him who prospers in his way,

because of the man who carries out wicked schemes.

Cease from anger, and forsake wrath;

fret not yourself; it leads to evildoing.

For evildoers will be cut off,

but those who wait for the Lord, they will inherit the land.

--Psalm 37:6-9

Day 268

10/31/15

Well, there is nothing to celebrate on our anniversary this year. We're separated, getting a divorce, not speaking and our affairs are destroyed.

And yet, I have a little seedling of joy growing in my heart! And if I will allow it, I know the Lord will continue to refocus me to what He is doing. He's drawing my eyes away from dwelling in this earthly comparison of action and intentions, and drawing me near to Himself!

Thank You, Lord; measuring with Your yardstick is a safe place for me. My life is in Your hands.

And though you have not seen Him, you love Him,

and though you do not see Him now,

but believe in Him,

you greatly rejoice with joy inexpressible and full of glory,

obtaining as the outcome of your faith the salvation of your souls.

--1 Peter 1:8-9

Day 269

11/23/15

Friends are still hearing the news, and they just can't believe this has happened. Actually, I still can't believe it either and I am living this thing! And I hadn't counted on the trauma of reliving these circumstances over and over. Yuck!

But I thank the Lord, He is most certainly willing to walk with me, especially in the trauma. When I think of His suffering, my path is so much easier. And so much of the sting of pain in my own life is removed!

Now I know the Lord saves His anointed;

He will answer him from His holy heaven,

with the saving strength of His right hand.

--Psalm 20:6

Day 270

11/17/15

Today is "his" birthday. Today I am thankful for "him" being born because that single thing has changed the landscape of my life. God has used "him" as a tool to bring me to a sweet place with the Lord.

And I am even thankful for the pain "he" has caused by "his" sin. That pain is shaping me into the person I am today, one with compassion for others. It is reminding me of all those who have endured and even blossomed through the pain in their lives.

Thank You, Lord, for Your graciousness; it is molding me into Your image!

And God is able to make all grace abound to you,

so that always having all sufficiency in everything,

you may have an abundance for every good deed.

--2 Corinthians 9:8

Day 271

11/8/15

Today I am thankful for purple flannel sheets! It has gotten a little chilly at night and I am cold!

Since I left home and only took some things, I find that I'm constantly saying, "I have that, but it's locked in my house." But the sheets—I remembered packing them away. Last night I looked for them and there they were, clean, wrapped in plastic, and purple. I'm all about the purple! I had thought I grabbed the green ones we had in the guestroom!

I thank You, Lord; although it often feels like my land is parched and desolate because of what I've lost, You keep me safe in Your arms.

Rule #7   God's arm is long enough to walk with me every step. God loves!

> *But godliness actually is a means of great gain*
>
> *when accompanied by contentment.*
>
> *For we have brought nothing into the world,*
>
> *so we cannot take anything out of it either.*
>
> *If we have food and covering,*
>
> *with these we shall be content.*
>
> *--1 Timothy 6:6-8*

Day 272

12/10/15

When you have major surgery…other things get smaller. And you start to think about what is really important.

Thank You, Lord; You have kept me safe! You are meeting my needs! You have healed me in so many ways! Thank You, Lord; You have helped me to face all kinds of pain and to even rejoice in it!

Behold, God is my helper;
the Lord is the sustainer of my soul.
--Psalm 54:4

Day 273

8/9/16

There is no accounting for what God will do in another person's life. We may recognize what's happening in their life. We can pray for them and ask God to speak to them. God can illuminate to us their sin and the untruths they are living. But we absolutely cannot change their life or their mind. Only God can change a life!

This is where I was caught and spinning around like a whirlpool. But what I finally realized is that God was working in me whether my husband would listen to Him or not!

Thank You, Lord; You never cease to work in our lives to bring about Your glory. The whole world is rushing by, straining against You, but You are still standing by waiting for us.

I can be with You; You are here with me! Thank You, Lord!

For as the rain and the snow come down from heaven,

and do not return there without watering the earth,

and making it bear and sprout

and furnishing seed to the sower and bread to the eater;

so shall My word be which goes forth from My mouth;

it shall not return to Me empty without accomplishing what I desire,

and without succeeding in the matter for which I sent it.

--Isaiah 55:10-11

Day 274

6/25/15

It is easy to spin out with emotions of fear and anxiety; I am out of control!

As soon as these feelings bubble up, I'm taking them captive. These feelings tell me what I'm believing about God, myself and the situation. For me, it's mostly about my thinking that God is not powerful enough to take care of me!

God most certainly is more powerful than "him" and "his" shenanigans!

Thank You, Lord, for reminding me over and over that You care for me! I see it so often in the birds. You care for the little birds; how much more do you care for me?

Look at the birds of the air,

that they do not sow, neither do they reap,

nor gather into barns,

and yet your heavenly Father feeds them.

Are you not worth much more than they?

--Matthew 6:26

Day 275

8/19/15

    There are random memories coming through my mind. They include so many little things that we used to do together. Sometimes the memories are bitter sweet; sometimes they bring relief. Either way, it's an opportunity to see what God wants to do through this place in my life. I'm holding Your hand, Dear Lord!

    Thank You, Lord, for being with me through pain and sweet memories. Thank You, Lord; You were there with us when we made the memories, and You will show me what to do with those memories now. You are sweet, Lord, and gentle!

The Lord is gracious and merciful;

slow to anger

and great in lovingkindness.

--Psalm 145:8

Day 276

10/27/15

    I have been in a bit of a tizzy…what if… (You always know to take that thought captive right away!) "What if I pick another 'wrong' guy?"

    It is a real temptation to start looking around for the next one, someone to love me, to tell me "You are okay!" I'm so thankful for some Godly wisdom from a friend!

#1 I'm still legally married.

#2 I need at least a year for healing time to work through things with the Lord. That's a year after the divorce is final.

#3 And most importantly, God has set my feet on a new path, walking closely with Him. I can trust Him to provide guidance!

Rule #4 God will show you what you need to see. God sees!

    If He has a man for me to share my life with, He will work it out! Thank You Lord, for watching out for me! Your love never fails!

I will bless the Lord who has counseled me;

Indeed, my mind instructs me in the night.

I have set the Lord continually before me;

because He is at my right hand, I will not be shaken.

Therefore my heart is glad,

and my glory rejoices;

my flesh also will dwell securely.

--Psalm 16:7-9

Day 277

7/6/15

It is a true statement--I am wounded! I don't always think of myself that way but it's true! So, whenever someone does something a little bit hurtful, it quickly becomes a very big thing. And almost before I can run to the Lord, my emotions turn my boat over!

Help me, Lord, to hear Your voice over any other. Help me to lean into You instead of following my own way. I want to entrust myself into Your strong arms! Thank You, Lord, for being strong!

Who is the King of glory?
The Lord is strong and mighty,
the Lord mighty in battle.
—Psalm 24:8

Day 278

9/24/15

I have had some trouble accepting this path that the Lord has given me to follow! I just keep saying, "This is not what I wanted." But I can see that this is where God has directed me and He has shown me His provision so many times along the way.

And I can see that my focus is looking back to what was, and I believe God wants me to look forward with Him!

Rule #4   God will show you what you need to see. God sees!

Thank You, Lord; You do see. You can see all of my life, even the moments I haven't lived through yet. You know what direction I should go and You will show me and walk with me all throughout the journey!

But the path of the righteous is like the light of dawn,

that shines brighter and brighter until the full day.

--Proverbs 4:18

Day 279

11/1/15

I can see the look in people's faces—sometimes they seem tired of hearing that I am having a tough day. Their eyes glaze over when I mention the struggle!

That can happen when you are living out loud, being authentic. People may be uncomfortable with your pain and suffering. But I can be okay in the midst of their discomfort, because my part in this Christian life is to walk with the Lord in truth and light.

Rule #3   No one gets to say who I am but God. God says!

Thank You, Lord; I am safe and secure in You. I may feel pain and express it, but I am still in You and You are in me!

For you were formerly darkness,

but now you are light in the Lord;

walk as children of light.

--Ephesians 5:8

Day 280

11/25/15

A year ago the one I loved disappeared for five hours on Thanksgiving Day. I was so trusting, after all isn't that what marriage is built on? So, I just sat there at "his" sister's home waiting, and watching and wondering what was going on? That might have been the first time I let the bad stuff be seen by others.

This year I am a lot more brave. This year I'm so thankful for a whole year with the Lord! This year I said, "No, I'm not covering up for "you" anymore. I'm telling the truth!"

Thank You, Lord, for a brand new holiday, a day to be thankful for who You are. You are beautiful and faithful and You are my redeemer!

Better is a dry morsel and quietness with it

than a house full of feasting with strife.

--Proverbs 17:1

Day 281

11/24/15

It's two days until Thanksgiving and I have so much to be thankful for! I have survived this awful, terrible year and God has kept me safe.

I can truly say that I'm not filled with anger and bitterness. God has guarded my heart from those things. I have been surrounded by a great cloud of witnesses; people who have held me up this year. I am so grateful!

I have no idea what's coming next but God knows and is with me. And whatever is ahead…Thank You, Lord!

But thanks be to God,

who gives us victory through our Lord Jesus Christ.

Therefore, my beloved brethren,

be steadfast, immovable, always abounding in the work of the Lord,

knowing that your toil is not in vain in the Lord.

--1 Corinthians 15:57-58

Day 282

6/26/15

It keeps running through my mind, "When I get my own place, I'll do…" This holding pattern is cumbersome! Thank You, Lord; I have a place to stay, a roof and a place to do my life's work. You are providing this in a miraculous way.

But God, I still want a place of my own. I want to be settled and to put up my things and live. Please remind me, Lord, this is where I am today and my tomorrow is Your business!

For indeed, in this house we groan,

longing to be clothed with our dwelling from heaven;

--2 Corinthians 5:2

Day 283

6/25/15

And when you are just too tired, a little worried and distracted, and anxious… that is the perfect time for the Lord! Thank You, Lord, for meeting me again!

Thou art my hiding place;

Thou dost preserve me from trouble;

Thou dost surround me with songs of deliverance.

I will instruct you in the way which you should go;

I will counsel you with My eye upon you…

be glad in the Lord

and rejoice you righteous ones,

and shout for joy all you who are upright in heart.

--Psalm 32:1 and 8 and 11

Day 284

11/19/15

Today I am thankful for a patchwork quilt. It kept me so warm and cozy last night that I didn't wake up; I slept straight through the night! Getting a full night's sleep has been a problem this year.

This quilt was made by my seventh and eighth grade girls Sunday school class and a sweet mom. It was their wedding gift to us.

So along with the grief I'm feeling over our broken marriage, I see these sweet sayings and scriptures, as well as their faces and names. This morning I was comforted by the words of God on the quilt: "God is faithful," "God is my strength," "God bears all things." They wrote and sewed and painted God's words over me.

Thank You, Lord, that You can and will use Your word to show us the way. I'm thankful that You comfort and love us.

Be gracious to me, O God,

be gracious to me,

for my soul takes refuge in Thee;

and in the shadow of Thy wings I will take refuge,

until destruction passes by.

--Psalm 57:1

Day 285

11/27/15

Through some extraordinary circumstances, I have broken my left arm. This is my writing hand! For this it is hard to be grateful!

But it is bringing to me an outpouring of love, prayers and service! Thank You, Lord, for meeting my needs once again!

Since I am afflicted and needy, let the Lord be mindful of me;

Thou art my help and my deliverer,

do not delay, O My God.

--Psalm 40:17

Day 286

11/25/15

And here it is—Thanksgiving is tomorrow. I've finished my work, and I am alone! It feels so weird that I got comfortable living in the garbage. I was so used to the stress, the yelling and wondering what "he" was doing that now I actually miss it.

Teach me, Lord, to glory in the truth, to find joy in Your great gift of love. May I grow comfortable in Your unknown plans!

I remember the days of old.

I meditate on all Thy doings;

I muse on the work of Thy hands,

I stretch out my hand to Thee,

my soul longs for Thee, as a parched land.

--Psalm 143:6

Day 287

8/25/15

It's so funny that a year ago I was reading the same thing! I've been going through a Bible study book and the chapter is on expectations, anger, and forgiveness. Maybe I'll make this something to do every year at this time.

A year ago this chapter would have scared me. Today I am comforted! The Lord has done so many things in a year.

Thank You, Lord; I can see behind me all the ways You have met me. I can look without regret. Thank You, Lord, for showing me how You have changed my anger to joy so many times. Please, Lord, continue to be a balm for the pain!

And those who know Thy name will put their trust in Thee;

for Thou, O Lord,

hast not forsaken those who seek Thee.

--Psalm 9:10

Day 288

11/30/15

How many days can I wear the same tank top without going insane? This is not a question I ever thought about asking. The answer is six days. ☺ I fell and broke my arm. It's in a sling and a body wrap, so I've been stuck in these clothes for six days.

Thank You, Lord, that You have met me here in this broken place! You have not blinked! You are meeting needs even before I can think to ask!

Make me to hear joy and gladness,

let the bones which Thou has broken rejoice.

Hide Thy face from my sins,

and blot out all my iniquities.

Create in me a clean heart, O God,

and renew a steadfast spirit within me.

--Psalm 51:8-10

Day 289

4/29/16

It's with a lot of dread that I'm planning to go to our house for some things I had to leave behind. I really don't want to go, but there are things that I still want.

I really want to stop thinking about it and close the door. May I close the door, Lord? Will You close the door?

I will follow You no matter what! Open the door, close the door, whichever way You want, I will do what You say, Lord!

> *Then the Lord opened the eyes of Balaam,*
> *and he saw the angel of the Lord standing in the way*
> *with his drawn sword in his hand;*
> *and he bowed all the way to the ground.*
> *And the angel of the Lord said to him,*
> *why have you struck your donkey these three times?*
> *Behold, I have come out as an adversary,*
> *because your way was contrary to me.*
> *But the donkey saw me and turned aside from me,*
> *I would surely have killed you just now, and let her live.*
> *And Balaam said to the angel of the Lord,*
> *"I have sinned, for I did not know that you were standing*
> *in the way against me.*
> *Now then, if it is displeasing to you, I will turn back."*
> *--Numbers 22:31-34*

Rule #4   God will show you what you need to see. God sees!

Day 290

5/30/16

It's been a month since I wrote that I was going to the house to get my things. Don't be surprised; it didn't happen. Now the word is, "Her things are in storage, "I" will give the key to my lawyer." What? I could have gone to storage six months ago if this storage space with all my things actually exists!

Oh Dear Lord, wow! I am so tired of the games and manipulations! Thank You, Lord; You still know what's going on!

Rule #1 Don't try to figure it out…it could hurt your brain. God knows!

…and to ask that you may be filled with the knowledge of His will

in all spiritual wisdom and understanding,

so that you may walk in a manner worthy of the Lord…

--Colossians 1:9b-10a

Day 291

5/29/16

I'm still wondering about this vengeance and recompense. What form will it take? I suspect that I have been looking in the wrong direction all this time. Maybe it's really like so many other of God's principles—right in front of us and waiting to be walked in, lived in, and breathed out to others.

Thank You, Lord; You make the rough smooth and the difficult simple. You are amazing!

Encourage the exhausted, and strengthen the feeble.

Say to those with a palpitating heart,

"Take courage, fear not.

Behold Your God will come with vengeance;

the recompense of God will come,

but He will save you."

--Isaiah 35:3-4

Day 292

7/30/16

> *For consider Him who has endured such hostility*
> *by sinners against Himself,*
> *so that you may not grow weary and lose heart.*
>
> *--Hebrews 12:3*

I think I have been losing heart over the last few weeks. Don't get me wrong; I am really so thankful that God has brought me through these treacherous times on the journey.

But these last two weeks, I have hit another stone wall; it is the biggest one yet. I cannot move it, I cannot go around it, over it or anything!

I'm afraid; I have sat at the foot of the rocks and moaned and cried until I am done in! Oh Lord, I'm waiting here for You to change my heart in any way that pleases You! I love You, Lord! Show me Your deep, real peace, even when all I can do is wait!

Day 293

4/27/16

It is quiet. I'm waiting on You again, Lord! There's a feeling that it's time for it all to be over but…not quite yet!

Thank You, Lord; each step in this journey has been with You. In this I have learned to pray and talk with You each moment! I have learned to leave the swirling thoughts and come to Your arms. I have learned that You are working so many times when I cannot see or imagine.

Dear Lord, please keep me working in all You have shown me!

Rule #4   God will show you what you need to see. God sees!

As a result, we are no longer to be children,

tossed here and there by waves and carried about

by every wind of doctrine,

by the trickery of men, by craftiness in deceitful scheming;

but speaking the truth in love,

we are to grow up in all respects into Him, who is head,

even Christ, from whom the whole body,

being fitted and held together by that which every joint supplies,

according to the proper working of each individual part,

causes the growth of the body for the building up of itself in love.

--Ephesians 4:14-16

Day 294

12/7/15

Not much sleep…up early and surgery on my broken arm later today. I'm not feeling much like being thankful! Help me, Lord!

> *I will say to God my rock,*
> *"Why hast Thou forsaken me?*
> *Why do I go mourning because of the oppression of the enemy?"*
> *As the shattering of my bones, my adversaries revile me,*
> *while they say to me all day long, "Where is your God?"*
> *Why are you in despair, O my soul?*
> *And why have you become disturbed within me?*
> *Hope in God, for I shall yet praise Him,*
> *the help of my countenance, and my God.*
>
> *--Psalm 42:9-11*

Day 295

7/9/16

Last night at midnight my name changed. This was such an important thing to me. I come from a good, honorable name, from hardworking, honest people who endure!

This feels like a fresh start, even though I've had so many fresh starts in the past two years--this is the biggest one. It has really gone a long way to closing the door, and to shaking off the dust to walk in the truth!

Thank You, Dear Lord. When you died for me, You gave me a fresh start and a new name! You enveloped me in You and I became new. Thank You, Lord! I am Your child, You have called me by name!

A good name is to be more desired than great riches,

favor is better than silver and gold.

--Proverbs 22:1

Day 296

12/19/15

This week the Lord took care of a $1,312 bill. I am so thankful!! It was the bill for the ambulance when I fell and broke my arm. The home where I fell did not cover the ambulance ride since I don't live there. But because my landlord pays the fee on his water bill, I am covered. I still can't believe it!

I think I have lived my entire adult life thinking that if you don't have the money to pay for it, don't do it! During this time I've had to just surrender it up to God. That's pretty tough for this very practical girl!

Thank You, Lord, for meeting our every need. For making light when I can't see. Thank You that Your faithfulness is not dependent upon my understanding! You make a way and You show us how to walk in it!

For Thou dost light my lamp;

the Lord my God illuminates my darkness.

For by Thee I can run through a troop;

and by my God I can leap over a wall!

--Psalm 18:28-29

Day 297

7/12/15

Just when I think I'm doing well another layer of tears start randomly coming.

The sweetest man at church came up to me today and asked where my husband was. I had to say again for the hundredth time, "we are getting divorced; "he" has left me for another woman."

Not only did "he" leave me, break our marriage and pretend "he" wasn't doing anything wrong, but "he" tried to hurt me because I said, "No more." And now I get the horrible task of answering questions like these and telling all of our friends why "he" has disappeared from our lives.

Thank You, Lord, for friends who care so much and are brave enough to broach the subject. Thank You for always being with me each step of the way! I know You have a plan!

But the salvation of the righteous is from the Lord;

He is their strength in time of trouble.

And the Lord helps them,

and delivers them;

He delivers them from the wicked,

and saves them,

because they take refuge in Him.

--Psalm 37:39-40

Day 298

2/22/16

Even after a whole year has passed, I still have times when I'm thinking, "what's "he" doing, why is "he" being so contrary about the end of our marriage?" Swimming around in all of the mess is truly exhausting.

Rule #6   Lay down the *why*. God understands!

Thank You, Lord; You are here with me, reminding me of the truth. You love me; You are working in this! Praise Your holy name!

But Thou, O Lord, be not far off; O Thou my help, hasten to my assistance.

Deliver my soul from the sword, my only life from the power of the dog.

Save me from the lion's mouth;

and from the horns of the wild oxen Thou dost answer me.

--Psalm 22:19-21

Day 299

6/23/15

There are little moments brought to us by the Lord—special little happenings in a day. Today for me it was a lady who took my storage locker payment! In our short conversation, I got to share all the Lord has been doing in my heart and she shared about her own pain!

I had not imagined the agony of having my heart stomped. She made it seem not so horrible but just part of a real life. Thank You, Lord; today You used someone with skin, heart and courage to remind me that You are always with me. In the good, in the pain, rain or shine, You never sleep or blink or miss any part of my life!

I will lift up my eyes to the mountains;

from where shall my help come?

My help comes from the Lord, who made heaven and earth.

He will not allow your foot to slip;

He who keeps you will not slumber.

Behold, He who keeps Israel will neither slumber nor sleep.

--Psalm 121:1-4

Day 300

3/19/15

I have spent plenty of time trying to convince myself that this is really happening. It is totally against every fiber of my being; I have no control. I am caught in a swirl of lies and deceit with no way to escape.

Thank You, Lord; I have mostly gotten past that stage. You are showing me the quick truth. For all of the many lies You brought the truth along quickly so that I could see and follow You!

Rule #2 Don't dialogue with the devil. God is truth!

Only fear the Lord and serve Him in truth with all your heart;

for consider what great things He has done for you.

--1 Samuel 12:24

Day 301

8/10/15

When you walk with the Lord, there is safety, companionship and moments of pure joy! Sometimes it feels scary and lonely, but I have only to call out to Him and He is just a moment away!

Oh Lord, please keep training me to call out for You! Please guard my heart from the spin out and getting weighted down with worry! Just a tiny little thought can get in and if unchecked, it can grow into a mountain of worry. Please Lord, help me to keep checking in with You. Guard my thoughts!

...in addition to all,

taking up the shield of faith

with which you will be able to extinguish

all the flaming missiles of the evil one.

--Ephesians 6:16

Day 302

6/25/15

The sweet friends that You are sending my way should not be taken for granted! I just keep thinking of the 'great cloud of witnesses' from the Bible. I have so many friends who You have led to walk beside me, praying all the way.

Thank You, Lord, for Your people who love You and who lift me up, care for me and are committed to me! Thank You, Lord; they are Your hands and feet for me!

For You have delivered my soul from death,

indeed my feet from stumbling,

so that I may walk before God in the light of the living.

--Psalm 56:13

Day 303

11/10/15

It is such a joy when you pray for something and the Lord shows an answer quickly.

I had prayed that the Lord would release me from having to look around for "his" vehicle in order to avoid seeing "him." And within 48 hours, there was an answer. Thank You, Lord; I heard that "he" bought a different car and I have no idea what it looks like. What a relief!

This is a small way for the Lord to give me an opportunity to let go of this. I don't need to be worrying about where "he" is or if I'll be seeing "him." In reality although, "he" works near a store that I frequent I have only seen "him" there one time!!

Thank You, Lord; You heard my heart and provided an answer right away. And now I can go to the grocery store without scanning the parking lot. This small thing is very big to me.

Thou hast relieved me in my distress;
Be gracious to me and hear my prayer.
--Psalm 4:1

Day 304

12/20/15

Today as I'm walking out of the church, it hits me; it's the Sunday before Christmas and my husband has left me. I'm alone… There was just a moment where I felt sorry for myself; then I sighed, choked back a couple of tears and said, "Thank You, Lord."

Thank You, Lord; this is where I am with You. You love me and You are keeping me safe. You love me!

Thy hands made me and fashioned me;

give me understanding, that I may learn Thy commandments.

May those who fear Thee see me and be glad,

because I wait for Thy word.

--Psalm 119:73-74

Day 306

8/12/15

As I walked past my car, I noticed that on one of my front tires, I could see the wires. That is not good!

The next day I am off to buy a new tire. A sweet friend/family called the tire store to get me in and when I get there, they have arranged to buy a second tire for me.

Thank You, Lord; You provided double today. You kept me safe and You gave me two new tires. Thank You for watching out for Your babies!

Come see the works of God,

who is awesome in His deeds toward the sons of men.

--Psalm 66:5

Day 307

6/17/15

I never wanted to believe it was true. Why would I? I was married and walking with the Lord. I thought "he" was too. We had some problems, but I thought I knew how to do marriage!

Then things started to happen; things that I couldn't believe. It took a long time to even imagine that "he" was developing a relationship with "her." In fact, by the time I realized something might possibly be developing, I think "they" were already well into the relationship!

It will not ever make sense to me. I can bash my head against a wall every day to try to understand; but I think I'll need to just lay it at the feet of Jesus, over and over!

Thank You, Lord; You know it all, You love me and You are here with me. You give me life!

Rule #1   Don't try to figure it out…it could hurt your brain. God knows!

Rule #6   Lay down the *why*. God understands!

> *Only the Lord give you discretion and understanding,*
>
> *and give you charge over Israel,*
>
> *so that you may keep the law of the Lord your God.*
>
> *Then you will prosper,*
>
> *if you are careful to observe the statutes and the ordinances*
>
> *which the Lord commanded Moses concerning Israel.*
>
> *--1 Chronicles 22:12-13*

Day 308

6/27/15

I have this expectation to wake up in the morning and feel happy! But I can't remember when I woke up with a feeling like that!

Thank You, Lord, for this day. Thank You for all You're going to do in it. Please remind me that this is Your day. You have given it to me. Thanks for showing me, just now, that I've been taking responsibility for my days. That is wrong. You are in charge of the days; it's not for me to number them and judge them and fix them! Thank You, Lord, for the day!

"This is the day which the Lord has made;

let us rejoice and be glad in it."

--Psalm 118:24

Day 309

7/14/15

I can hardly wait to step into the next part of the journey. That desire produces thoughts of what is ahead, what's going to happen, and where I am going? In the past, and maybe even earlier today, I would start "planning it forward," which means I would be planning out the steps ahead! There is nothing wrong with planning except when you're doing it to feel safe! That has been my habit.

These days I'm having to lay that down to the Lord! Thank You, Lord; I don't know Your plans for me, nor do I know which way to go or how to act when I get there. Thank You that I can entrust each of my days to You. You have a plan and are working in me!

The steps of a man are established by the Lord;

and He delights in his way.

When he falls, he shall not be hurled headlong;

because the Lord is the One who holds his hand.

--Psalm 37:23-24

Day 310

8/4/15

We have power in our tongues. We have power to speak love and grace and power to wound. And each moment, we have a heart choice which of these our words will accomplish. I think the words have to come from our relationship with the Lord.

When I am struggling with who I am in Him, I am certain to put myself first! When I am on the throne of my life, I will often wound with my words!

Thank You, Lord, for showing me that my daily life choices have consequences. Please remind me to cling to You moment by moment. Remind me that I am not the lord of my life. I know that You, Lord, are my guide for each step! Please keep me hearing Your voice!

In my trouble I cried to the Lord,

and He answered me.

Deliver my soul, O Lord,

from lying lips,

from a deceitful tongue.

--Psalm 120:2

Day 311

4/6/16

It's just three days until the Pretrial Hearing. I can sense that God is preparing me for this great adventure! I really have no idea what is going to happen at court! I do know, however, that God is big, so, so big. And I know that He is working and will be with me that day.

Thank You, Lord; I can entrust myself to You each day. I love You, Lord; You are magnificent in all Your ways!

For Thou hast maintained my just cause;
Thou dost sit on the throne judging righteously.
--Psalm 9:4

A rascally witness makes a mockery of justice,
and the mouth of the wicked spreads iniquity.
Judgments are prepared for scoffers,
and blows for the back of fools.
--Proverbs 19:28-29

Day 312

6/7/16

I'm really not feeling that thankful today. After over a year of trying to retrieve some of the things I left behind, no progress has been made! In fact, I would say it feels like I'm going backwards.

"He" gave a key to "his" lawyer. "He" said it is for a storage unit that contains my belongings. But of course, I can't get in at the storage place without having my name on the list or the key code for the gate. Going backwards!

And I know full well that there will probably just be a lot of garbage in there, assuming the key actually fits the lock!

Okay, Lord, I must lay this at Your feet. I have cried enough tears! "He" has no power over me. You are God; You alone! You want my highest and best good all the time.

Rule #8   God, indeed, has more power that everyone and everything. God is!

The Lord will protect you from evil;

He will keep your soul.

The Lord will guard your going out

and your coming in from this time forth

and forever.

--Psalm 121:7-8

Day 313

6/7/1

On a very personal note…let me begin with—"God is Big." And I am resolved to walk with Him forever!

That being said, there are days like today that bump up again my resolve in a big way. You know the days, filled with moments where you're kind of beat up and reeling, with drops of sweat and tears running off your face. And there's a heart cry without any sounds! The people in the car next to you are staring. You just know they're thinking, "Oh my goodness, quick, throw her a box of tissues!!" That's the day I've had.

But Thank You, Lord; I didn't go hungry or naked. I'm safe and no one ran me over. I laughed a couple of times; I kicked satan in the teeth and I lived to walk through another day. And God is still Big! In fact, He might just be a little bigger to me now than when I woke up this morning.

And this has not been my worst day ever. Thank You, Lord! I can't wait to see what Your tomorrow will bring!

Then Joshua said to the people,

"Consecrate yourselves,

for tomorrow the Lord will do wonders among you."

--Joshua 3:5

Day 314

2/14/16

Well, I lived through the first Valentine's Day without "him." I went to church to hear God's word and that was awesome! I survived the weekend without feeling sorry for myself.

I'm closing the door and having a fresh start! Thank You, Lord, for these new chances to hold tight to You and Thank You for Your endurance!

And He said to me,

"It is done,

I am the Alpha and the Omega, the beginning and the end.

I will give to the one who thirsts from the spring

of the water of life without cost.

He who overcomes shall inherit these things,

and I will be his God

and he will be My son."

--Revelation 21:6-7

Day 315

8/16/15

And then there was today… Another wrinkle and I don't know how to deal with it. Another doubt--have I done enough? I'm thinking that these questions will always be with me!

Thankfully, as long as the questions, doubts and trials go on, God is longer still! My God, is so is awesome that He stays with us through it all!

Rule #7 God's arm is long enough to walk with me every step. God loves!

Thank You, Lord; my life has not taken You by surprise. You aren't afraid of the wrinkles that crop up in my life! You, Dear Lord, love me and all Your babies so much. You are watching with joy at the sweet dependence we have on You!

But He led forth His own people like sheep,

and guided them in the wilderness like a flock;

and He led them safely, so that they did not fear;

but the sea engulfed their enemies.

--Psalm 78:52-53

Day 316

10/24/15

This week my house was broken into and they took a lot of my possessions. I'm finding that thoughts of self-pity and worry are trying to overcome me. I keep thinking of Job and how so many struggles were heaped on him. And I think—how much further down can I go?

Thank You, Lord, my life is not measured by possessions. I could be anywhere and still have my most valuable possession. No one can snatch me out of Your hand!!

> "Behold, I have inscribed you on the palms of My hands;
> your walls are continually before Me.
> Your builders hurry;
> your destroyers and devastators will depart from you."
> "For your waste and desolate places,
> and your destroyed land--
> surely now you will be too cramped for the inhabitants,
> And those who swallowed you will be far away."
> "They will bow down to you with their faces to the earth,
> and lick the dust of your feet;
> and you will know that I am the Lord;
> those who hopefully wait for Me will not be put to shame."
> --Isaiah 49:16 and 19 and 23b

Day 317

7/3/15

It was a tough day, an anniversary of a tough day last year! I suppose that I'll be having some more of them as the Lord makes a new life! Thank You, Lord; you are wise enough to help me navigate these trying times! You are enough to walk with me every step of the way!

Rule #7   God's arm is long enough to walk with me every step. God loves!

Whom have I in heaven but Thee?

And besides Thee,

I desire nothing on earth.

My flesh and my heart may fail;

but God is the strength of my heart

and my portion forever.

--Psalm 73:25-26

Day 318

8/25/15

From my journal, November 28, 2014:

"I know You love me! I know You sent Your Son; He died for my sin. He Loves Me! And You sent Your Spirit to love me, to live in me, and to show me the way to go!"

Thank You, Lord, that Your love is enough, always holding me, all the time! I will ever trust You. I will glorify You. You are God, Keeper of my soul.

I love You, Lord; please keep my eyes focused on You!

O Lord, Thou art my God;

I will exalt Thee,

I will give thanks to Thy name;

For Thou hast worked wonders,

plans formed long ago,

with faithfulness.

--Isaiah 25:1

Day 319

10/30/15

Tomorrow is our Trunk or Treat at church. For years my sweet friend and I have had a Fishing Booth. It consisted of a big refrigerator box painted to look like ocean. The kids would throw the fishing line over with their cane pole; we would put a piece of candy on the clothespin and throw it back. One of the physical things I lost this year was my fishing booth! This makes me sad!

Thank You, Lord; I get to make a new game! It's going to be a Bean Bag Toss! But I'll miss my friend as she does her new thing…time with family!

Dear Lord, please help my heart take courage as I embrace new things! Remind me that I am there to smile and greet strangers whom You love and want to touch. And thank you, Lord; I have my clown costume to wear!

Rejoice always; pray without ceasing;

in everything give thanks;

for this is God's will for you in Christ Jesus.

--1 Thessalonians 5:16-18

Day 320

12/5/15

The second thing people say to me is: "Is "he" still with "her?"

I guess this is supposed to be some measuring stick? It seems like they are inferring that if "he" were NOT still with "her," then that would really change things! I'm finding that it's not so much about if "he" is still with "her." "She" is a product of deep sin. Much work with the Lord is the only solution I can see for that.

The Lord has spoken to my broken heart. And although my feelings still take me to "I love you" sometimes, the facts are clear in front of me!

Rule #4 God will show you what you need to see. God sees!

Thank You, Lord, for showing me what has taken place and what is still happening. Thank You for showing me that I can walk with You in truth. I can leave behind the lies and deceit. Please keep reaching out to "him," Lord. I pray that "he" will listen and turn back to You!

For now we see in a mirror dimly,

but then face to face;

now I know in part,

but then I will know fully

just as I also have been fully known.

--1 Corinthians 13:12

Day 321

8/28/16

You might be surprised when a day comes along that is not filled with thoughts of the hurt and pain. And soon you'll be able to rest, to take a breath, to let your heart take joy, courage, and love!

The flowers might look brighter. You'll hear birds singing and maybe see a cloud that makes you smile. A new life will become more and more visible! Let it in! Thank You, Lord, for Your beauty and remind me to see it, whenever I can!

Be strong,

and let your heart take courage,

all you who wait for the Lord.

--Psalm 31:24

Day 322

6/28/15

It feels like I'm trapped in an endless sea of pain. It's the worst feeling; it is as if I am holding on until there can be some closure or end. But I'm not certain if there will ever be an end to this pain and suffering.

Maybe that's not the point at all. We spend our whole lives trying to avoid pain and help others to avoid it. Does this really work?

Thank You, Lord; this is so confusing to me. Please teach me what to do with this pain!

Rule #1 Don't try to figure it out…it could hurt your brain. God knows!

And after you have suffered for a little,

the God of all grace,

who called you to His eternal glory in Christ,

will Himself perfect, confirm, strengthen and establish you.

--1 Peter 5:10

Day 323

1/2/16

It's time to say goodbye to 2015…the year I never wanted to go through! But God was with me every step of the way! There was pain, anguish, and too many tears. But God brought joy, laughter, peace and hope!

Thank You, Lord, that You are making the impossible way possible. And Thank You for lighting the way. Thank You for Your watch care and Your deep love for me!

Rule #7 God's arm is long enough to walk with me every step. God loves!

Many O Lord my God,

are the wonders which Thou has done,

and Thy thoughts toward us;

there is none to compare with Thee,

if I would declare and speak of them,

they would be too numerous to count.

--Psalm 40:5

Day 324

3/26/16

After a visit with my lawyer…it is so hard to know what to think next!

I want "him" to pay! I want "him" to be so utterly torn apart and repentant that "he" can do nothing but beg for forgiveness. I want "him" to be bankrupt, bruised, filthy, living on the street—I want "him" to pay! Then I will be happy. Then will it all be okay?

I want to yell at "him" until I lose my voice. I used to do that. My voice would be gone and I would be out of breath from yelling. And "he" would just stand there telling me lie after lie and seeming to be bewildered at my questions about where "he" had been!

BUT then I remember…Jesus paid it all! Thank You, Lord; You paid for our sin!

The way of the righteous is smooth;

O Upright One,

make the path of the righteous level.

Indeed, while following the way of Thy judgments,

O Lord, we have waited for Thee eagerly;

Thy name, even Thy memory,

is the desire of our souls.

--Isaiah 26:7-8

Day 325

7/12/15

It's a day of hope…that I can continue to move forward into my new life with You. I'm almost afraid to let the hope well up in me!

Thank You, Lord; my walk with You through this is not dependent on my performance! I can rest in You. As You bring the new life, I will walk in it! It will be difficult if You keep me here in this holding pattern, but this is Your business; my life is Yours. My time is in Your hands. I will not make this moving forward happen. You must propel me forward into today with Your grace and love and in Your time.

Rule #5   God's time is perfect! God endures!

There is an appointed time for everything.

And there is a time for every event under heaven…

…a time to weep, and a time to laugh;

a time to mourn, and a time to dance.

--Ecclesiastes 3:1 and 4

Day 326

7/16/15

This letting go is difficult.

A friend asked me about praying for "him," and it started me thinking. I have not been praying for "him," or even saying "his" name. I cannot! To pray for someone is to care for them. I feel that I need to stop caring for "him." To say someone's name is to know them. I need to stop knowing "him."

While this is true, the Lord has shown me that I have been purposing in my heart to do these things. He has also shown me that it is really His business to walk me through this letting go. He is the One who spoke to my heart and released me from the covenant I made.

Thank You, Lord; You will make a new life in me. You will show me how to live with You in Your world. You will direct me in this relationship and all others. You have knit my heart together with Yours! And You alone are in charge of unraveling this former life of mine and making it Your beautiful piece of art! Thank You, Lord!

Fear not,

for you will not be put to shame;

neither feel humiliated,

for you will not be disgraced;

but you will forget the shame of your youth,

and the reproach of your widowhood you will remember no more.

For your husband is your Maker, whose name is the Lord of Hosts;

and your Redeemer is the Holy One of Israel,

who is called the God of all the earth.

--Isaiah 54:4-5

Day 327

7/10/15

Each morning when I wake up I've been checking in with myself. "How do I feel today? Do I feel better, am I happy? Not yet, oh, no, I'm not happy yet! What am I going to do? How can I feel better?"

And so the day starts. I'm trying to arrange and order myself as to how I think I should be doing. I don't think it is what God wants! I just don't think God is that confusing!

Thank You, Lord; I'm not certain how to be or who I should be. Please, please keep teaching me to be just who You say I am! Please protect me from swimming in a mire of emotions and being tossed about by them. Thank You, Lord, for speaking to me!

Rule #3   No one gets to say who I am but God. God says!

I am the vine,

you are the branches;

he who abides in Me, and I in him,

he bears much fruit;

for apart from Me you can do nothing.

--John 15:5

Day 328

7/27/16

I am realizing again just how deeply this desire for vengeance is running through my life. I want justice!

So, I am still getting to lay it down before the Lord. And I get to make the choice again to follow Him instead of making my life happen in my own way.

Thank You, Lord; I can trust You because You are trustworthy!

From His dwelling place He looks out on all the inhabitants of the earth,

He who fashions the hearts of them all,

He understands all their works.

--Psalm 33:14-15

My soul waits for the Lord;

He is our help and our shield.

--Psalm 33:20

Day 329

2/5/16

Finally, after nearly a year, court is looming. It has taken so long to try to get things settled. I do not know how this next part is going to look and I feel scared!

I have tried to lay down my expectations about ever getting any money from our assets. But it's not really about the dollars!

The Lord is committed to take care of His children "according to His riches," which still isn't about the dollars! So, I'm in another place to trust the Lord. Lord, You are trustworthy. You are the same God today and forever.

In the same way God,

desiring even more to show to the heirs of the promise

the unchangeableness of His purpose,

interposed with an oath,

in order that by two unchangeable things

in which it is impossible for God to lie

we who have taken refuge would have strong encouragement

to take hold of the hope set before us.

This hope we have as an anchor of the soul,

a hope both sure and steadfast

and one which enters within the veil,

where Jesus has entered as a forerunner for us.

--Hebrews 6:17-20a

Day 330

2/9/16

Rule #2   Don't dialogue with the devil.   God is truth!

When the tiniest little bit of a thought that is destructive, fear-filled and untrue comes in, I must grab it up and run into the name of Jesus. That is the safe place where all such thoughts can have the light of truth shine on them. Then they can be disposed of right away.

This running to Jesus habit has been neglected in my life. But now, the bombarding with the thoughts is so much more intense and noticeable! Thank You, Lord; You are bringing the garbage to the surface so that You can shine Your light on it. Thank You for the darkness; it makes Your light bright!

Again therefore Jesus spoke to them, saying,

"I am the light of the world;

he who follows Me shall not walk in the darkness,

but shall have the light of life."

--John 8:12

Day 331

11/1/15

I have survived another anniversary event. But I'm a little upset with myself for not handling it better. I'm afraid I let the self-pity get the best of me.

Dear Lord, please always keep near to me. And keep me looking to You for strength in navigating sad things. Help me, Lord!

The Lord is my strength and song,

and He has become my salvation;

this is my God and I will praise Him;

my father's God,

and I will extol Him.

--Exodus 15:2

Day 332

2/29/16

As if the lies and cheating weren't enough, the pretending that I was imagining this whole thing has been awful. I feel like I'm going crazy!

Thank You, Lord; You have been my sanity all through this! You have kept my mind safe when all of it has engulfed me!

O Let the evil of the wicked come to an end,

but establish the righteous;

for the righteous, God tries the hearts and minds.

My shield is with God, who saves the upright in heart.

--Psalm 7:9-10

Day 333

7/16/15

Here's a story of God working in an extraordinary way!

I went to the church and told our Ministry Assistant that I was looking for a twin mattress and springs. She mentioned that she had driven by a demolished hotel that day where she saw piles of mattresses for free.

As I drive that way, praying, several things cross my mind. Hotels don't usually have twin beds and their beds probably wouldn't be that nice or clean! Then I think, "I can't fit anything bigger than a twin in my van. I can't even lift much either." So I pray, "Lord, You know these are a lot of 'ifs,' please make a way for me!"

I drive by a huge pile of hideous, filthy mattresses, which are the wrong sizes, but I notice the box springs are all in these zippered covers, away from dirt, etc.! Overwhelmed, I start to give up and drive away.

As I hesitate, a worker motions to me and says that there are more in another direction. I'm wondering if I should even get out of my car. Is a free mattress worth all this?

So, in I go, over piles of scrap metal and glass. And there it is, under a pile of mattresses, twenty feet away, one twin box spring, in the cover. Thank You, Lord! The man pulled it out of there and loaded it into my car!

Rule #4   God will show you what you need to see. God sees!

Thank You, Lord, for making the impossible, possible. The disgusting You make sweet!

When I remember You on my bed,

I meditate on You in the night watches,

for You have been my help,

and in the shadow of Your wings I sing for joy.

My soul clings to You;

Your right hand upholds me.

--Psalm 63:6-8

Day 334

10/30/16

The sting of the pain is starting to fade. The physical reactions still crop up sometimes; but thankfully, they are quickly going away. One thing I can say I have learned is to lean into the pain instead of pushing it down, ignoring it or swimming around in it.

As I am able, prompted by the Holy Spirit, to lay it before the Lord—He meets me there! When I am honest enough to say, "That hurts," God can come alongside. In fact, I've realized I am actually sharing in the sufferings of Christ.

Thank You, Lord; You did suffer. Your suffering paid the price for my sin. And it bought me freedom and eternal life!

Beloved, do not be surprised at the fiery ordeal among you,

which comes upon you for your testing,

as though some strange thing were happening to you;

but to the degree that you share the sufferings of Christ,

keep on rejoicing;

so that also at the revelation of His glory,

you may rejoice with exultation.

--1 Peter 4:12-13

Day 335

6/26/15

The *why* still comes to me sometimes but it's easier to stop it from overtaking me now. Thank You, Lord, for training!

These are all part of the new perspective:
1. I will probably never know why.
2. I have other things to think about, God can take care of me.
3. I have reason to hope in God's future for me.
4. It's all about Him, not about "him"!

Rule #6 Lay down the *why*. God understands!

As for you, my son Solomon,

know the God of your father,

and serve Him with a whole heart and a willing mind;

for the Lord searches all hearts,

and understands every intent of the thoughts.

If you seek Him, He will let you find Him;

but if you forsake Him, He will reject you forever.

--1 Chronicles 28:9

Day 336

7/16/15

I am not condemned because I was kind to the man I loved! That is what is ringing in my head today. If only I had been mean and gotten everything I could from the house when I left, then I would had what I need now. I had forgotten how many things you need to set up a household. I have no chest of drawers for my clothes.

Thank You, Lord; I have a place to set up house and a closet for clothes. Being able to rent a place is a miracle. Since I have been married for almost eighteen years and everything is in "his" name, I have almost no credit history. But God provided this sweet couple who agreed to take a chance on me.

Thank You, Lord; You know my every need and are waiting for the perfect time to fill the need! You are with me. And Thank You, Lord; I did not have to go out with fear, thinking that I must take everything I could and strip everything away from "him." You, Oh Lord, You are the one who takes care of us!!

"You need not fight in this battle;

station yourselves,

stand and see the salvation of the Lord on your behalf,

O Judah and Jerusalem."

Do not fear or be dismayed;

tomorrow go out to face them,

for the Lord is with you.

--2 Chronicles 20:17

Day 337

9/17/15

With each day, the terror gets a little less. I am feeling more able to put one foot in front of the other. And I'm less compelled by anxiety over what's coming next!

Thank You, Lord; You are bringing me through these days. I know You are working and walking with me.

I'm beginning to believe that You will work this out for Your good. I also believe I do have a purpose, that this present suffering is actually not for me, but for the people that You will be bringing into my life! Thank You, Lord, for some clarity!

> *"It is I who made the earth and created man upon it.*
>
> *I stretched out the heavens with My hands,*
>
> *and ordained all their hosts.*
>
> *I have aroused him in righteousness,*
>
> *and I will make all his ways smooth;*
>
> *he will build My city,*
>
> *and will let My exiles go free,*
>
> *without payment or reward,"*
>
> *says the Lord of hosts.*
>
> *--Isaiah 45:12-13*

Rule #7   God's arm is long enough to walk with me every step. God loves!

Day 338

1/21/16

I think I want to help people with things that have helped me. This is a human response. But truly, these things are all just tools with no real power in and of themselves. The real, life changing power is the Lord. The Holy Spirit works in us; He uses these tools to speak. All of God's creation cries out to tell us of His awesome power and grace!

Thank You, Lord; we have only to breathe in to see You working, we need only to relax in Your presence to be used by You! Please let them see Jesus in me!

What then?

Only that in every way,

whether in pretense or in truth,

Christ is proclaimed;

and in this, yes, I will rejoice.

--Philippians 1:18

Day 339

1/8/16

One more time…did I do enough? Thank You, Lord; You answer that question every time with "My beautiful child, I love you; you have done as I asked!" "You have clung to Me over and over; that is all I asked you to do!!"

> *He has told you, O Man,*
>
> *what is good;*
>
> *and what does the Lord require of you*
>
> *but to do justice,*
>
> *to love kindness,*
>
> *and to walk humbly with your God?*
>
> *--Micah 6:8*

But God…what if? These questions have self at their root. Please Lord; help me lay down self!

Rule #6 Lay down the *why*. God understands!

Day 340

6/22/15

> *"Vengeance is Mine, and retribution,*
>
> *in due time their foot will slip;*
>
> *for the day of their calamity is near,*
>
> *and the impending things are hastening upon them."*
>
> *--Deuteronomy 32:35*

I have had many times of wanting to hurt "him!" These feelings have been almost unbearable! Thank You, Lord; You have seen and not blinked at all that has been done to Your baby. And You, Lord, are completely able to put into motion Your principle; you reap what you sow! Thank You, Lord!

Rule #5   God's time is perfect. God endures!

Day 341

7/27/15

 Today, the one I am still married to on paper sent an email to hurt my business. I was just going along, walking with the Lord and this thing was happening behind my back.

 The person who got the email knew it was my husband reporting me for a "wrong." She contacted me; she already knew about my business through a friend. She said, "I just love your Sugar Cookies!" We laughed and laughed; then God used this to open a door to help my business!

 Thank You, Lord; You went before me today. You brought together some random pieces of my life and made a smooth path for me!

And as for you,

you meant evil against me,

but God meant it for good

in order to bring about this present result...

--Genesis 50:20

Day 342

10/22/15

God has been looking out for my best all along. I can see and believe that now. Looking back, there are so many times that stand out. These prove that God was with me.

This really helps for things that come up now. I can recall and am reminded of God's faithfulness! Thank You, Lord, for loving me enough to walk with me!

Rule #7 God's arm is long enough to walk with me every step. God loves!

Thank You for bringing to my mind all that You have done in my life.

Rule #4 God will show you what you need to see. God sees!

And Thank You for the courage to keep moving forward into Your tomorrow! I love You!

The Lord is your keeper;

the Lord is your shade on your right hand.

The sun will not smite you by day,

nor the moon by night.

The Lord will protect you from all evil;

He will keep your soul.

The Lord will guard your going out

and your coming in

from this time forth and forever.

--Psalm 121:5-8

Day 343

10/15/15

I am sometimes tempted to remove myself from my life. It's as if I think that relocating for a few days, will fix me. Ha ha, this is fraught with lies.

I cannot get away from God and what He is doing. It follows me wherever I am. And really, why would I want to leave the Lord? I am not lord of my life; He is! He knows everything about what's going on and how much I can handle. Thank the Lord! Running away has never solved anything for me—how about you??

The truth is anywhere I go and whatever I do, trying to get away from my life doesn't work. Leaning into it, offering it up to Him, being grateful for all that He is doing--that works. It gives me peace and joy and hope!

If I take the wings of the dawn,

if I dwell in the remotest part of the sea,

even there Thy hand will lead me,

and Thy right hand will lay hold of me.

--Psalm 139:9-10

Day 344

2/18/16

Another two months of waiting for the trial date is nearly unfathomable! Oh Dear Lord, it's been so long I'm not even certain of what I'm waiting for anymore!

Thank You, Lord; I know that Your desire for me is to walk more closely with You. You long to hold us in Your arms each moment of our days.

Thank You, Lord; You have given me the choice to choose You. I choose You, Lord, no matter what happens in my life!

>*And it will come about that whoever calls*
>
>*on the name of the Lord will be delivered;*
>
>*for on Mount Zion and in Jerusalem*
>
>*there will be those who escape,*
>
>*as the Lord has said,*
>
>*even among the survivors whom the Lord calls.*
>
>*--Joel 2:32*

Day 345

6/19/15

Making a new life seems weird! But yesterday I realized that I was thankful that I don't have to navigate "his" messes anymore! I have spent so much of our married life fixing things "he" did.

I don't have to try to look normal at church; I don't have to fix our finances when "he" overdrafts at the bank. And there's no more scrambling to force "him" to stay with me!

Thank You Lord, now I get to be with You. Thank You, Lord; You are creating a new life in me. I can't wait to see what You'll make of it!!

They will come and shout for joy on the height of Zion;

and they will be radiant over the bounty of the Lord,

over the grain and the new wine and the oil;

and over the young of the flock and the herd;

and their life will be like a watered garden,

and they will never languish again.

--Jeremiah 31:12

Day 346

9/18/15

I can only write this because of the work of God in my life…

I have been through many layers: grief, pain, vengeance, anger, joy, frustration, anguish, elation, relief, selfishness, confusion, spewing, hiding, questioning, resting, fighting, crying, thankfulness, grumbling, whining and joy. I've been through it all!

But now I know there is only one "layer" I want--resting in the Lord! Anything and everything can happen to me in this world, but my bottom line is the Lord. He is the only safe place!

These things I have spoken to you,

that in Me you may have peace.

In the world you will have tribulation,

but take courage;

I have overcome the world.

--John 16:33

Day 347

10/8/15

    Understanding and unpacking my emotions is difficult. We all have emotions, but I have not been certain what to do with mine for most of my life! Often I have wanted to ignore them! But today the Lord showed me in this verse that Jesus had feelings, so it must be okay to feel things. And in this passage, Jesus acted on His emotions. He felt compassion, and He fed them!

> *And seeing the multitudes,*
>
> *He felt compassion for them,*
>
> *because they were distressed and downcast*
>
> *like sheep without a shepherd.*
>
> *--Matthew 9:36*

    Truthfully, I think I've lived my life just going about, emoting and acting on it. I'm not certain this has really worked for me, nor has it honored the Lord! But I have been learning to use the emotions to tell me the lie I have believed. I feel anxious; therefore; I must believe that God is not big enough to meet my needs. Can it be that God wants to use the emotions He gave us to show us who He is and what He can do?

    Thank You, Lord, for emotions. Please help me understand what You want to do with mine. I know they are created by You.

Day 348

10/9/15

When will I know that I am finished with divorce and our life together? When will I be out of the fire? And out of the fire, what is this Christian life supposed to be? I'm not sure what steps to take next, Lord!

Beloved, do not be surprised at the fiery ordeal among you,

which comes upon you for your testing,

as though some strange thing were happening to you;

but to the degree that you share the sufferings of Christ,

keep on rejoicing;

so that also at the revelation of His glory,

you may rejoice with exultation.

--1 Peter 4:12-13

Day 349

11/10/15

I had grown concerned over the weekend when I realized that I didn't have money for my rent. Even though He has given me a small emergency fund, I don't want to spend it. I guess paying the rent could be called an emergency!

But the Lord blessed me yesterday when a friend/customer received a sewing project that I did for her. She gave me some extra dollars.

Thank You, Lord' for providing for me once again! You are the supplier of my needs.

Therefore, do not be like them;

for your Father knows what you need,

before you ask Him.

--Matthew 6:8

Day 350

12/5/15

    I am completely astounded by God's goodness! Today I stood up at our Ladies' Christmas Brunch to read about the Angels rejoicing. "Rejoice" is our theme.

    There I stood with my broken marriage and my broken arm. And above my head on the screen is the word, REJOICE! And today...I can rejoice, because of God's goodness!

How great is Thy goodness,

which Thou hast stored up for those who fear Thee,

which Thou hast wrought for those who take refuge in Thee,

before the sons of men!

--Psalm 31:19

Day 351

4/7/16

I feel afraid that You will make me walk down through another valley. I've walked through so many valleys this year—the year that I never wanted to go through!

Thank You, Lord; no matter how deep, no matter how long, no matter how hard it gets, I will follow You! I will walk through it with You. I love You, Lord!

For consider that the sufferings

of this present time

are not worthy to be compared

with the glory that is to be revealed to us.

--Romans 8:18

Rule #7   God's arm is long enough to walk with me every step. God loves!

Day 352

8/14/16

Last Sunday a sweet, dear friend confessed to me, "I do not understand why you are having to go through this." It was so wonderful, Lord, to have a chance to tell of the truth of Your goodness!

So, I told her two things. First, that since we love You, we will never make sense of this sin. And second, that because of this journey I'm on with You, Lord, I have a deeper walk. I can know a moment by moment relationship with You! That's a wonderful thing!

Thank You, Lord, for allowing me to go on this journey with You!

The Lord's lovingkindness indeed will never cease,

for His compassions never fail.

They are new every morning;

great is Thy faithfulness.

"The Lord is my portion," says my soul,

"Therefore I have hope in Him."

--Lamentations 3:22-23

Day 353

9/8/16

When I started this writing, I began crying out to the Lord in my journal. But very soon the Lord began to show me that there are many of us crying out!

If one person hears His voice and knows Him more, or if one enters into a life-long moment by moment love with the Lord, this will be a sweet thing!

I'm praying for you who are crying out. I am praying you will discover how real He is in your lives. Thank You, Lord--Jesus, Jesus, Jesus!

The Spirit of the Lord God is upon me,

because the Lord has anointed me

to bring good news to the afflicted;

He has sent me to bind up the brokenhearted,

to proclaim liberty to captives,

and freedom to prisoners;

to proclaim the favorable year of the Lord,

and the day of vengeance of our God;

to comfort all who mourn in Zion,

giving them a garland instead of ashes,

the oil of gladness instead of mourning,

the mantle of praise instead of a spirit of fainting.

So they will be called oaks of righteousness,

the planting of the Lord,

that He may be glorified.

--Isaiah 61:1-3

Day 354

8/14/16

I believe I am very close to the end of this journey with the Lord and with you who are traveling here too. And yet—it's really just the beginning! As we are able to step out into whatever God is doing new in us…it is really just another step along His path.

We don't really arrive in this thing called life in Christ. Or I guess the arriving part was when we said "Yes" to the Lord. "Yes," I believe You died for me. "Yes," I will give up my life to You. "Yes," I will follow You!

Then Jesus said to His disciples,

"If any one wishes to come after Me,

let him deny himself,

and take up his cross,

and follow Me."

"For whoever wishes to save his life shall lose it;

but whoever loses his life for My sake shall find it."

--Matthew 16:24-25

Day 355

4/27/16

I'm feeling some strong emotions because my marriage will be legally ended in a few days. I feel regret that my husband did the things that broke us from one into two.

Thank You, Lord; You hold all of us together in whatever relationship You choose. You knit hearts together. You show us and lead us and teach us how to love. You speak to us and say, "This is love."

Thank You, Lord, for loving me. Thank You for giving me this time with my husband. And Thank You for this new fresh start without "him."

Therefore be imitators of God,

as beloved children;

and walk in love,

just as Christ also loved you,

and gave Himself up for us,

an offering and a sacrifice to God

as a fragrant aroma.

--Ephesians 5:12

Day 356

4/10/16

Many things have been difficult in this journey. But the one thread running through this whole thing is that I have no control over any of it. So, in the midst of this uncontrollable mess of circumstances, I have had to choose. I can sit in the mess and stew or lay it all down for the Lord.

The laying down has been tough and annoying! I have to say over and over, "Lord, I can't fix this; I can't even figure it out."

Rule #1 Don't try to figure it out…it will hurt your brain. God knows!

But God knows. He knows. He knows! Thank You, Lord; You know everything. You have a solution that will bring You glory!

The conclusion, when all has been heard, is:

fear God and keep His commandments,

because this applies to every person.

Because God will bring every act to judgment,

everything which is hidden,

whether it is good or evil.

--Ecclesiastes 12:13-14

Day 357

7/21/15

Over and over…I have this lifelong pattern of rehearsing past conversations…just to see if I measured up to the standard. It's a constant battle with me and the Lord--to let go of the practice of self and let Him be my safety and security!

Thank You, Lord; You will be my sufficiency. You have measured me and found me to be Your precious child! I am covered by the blood of Your Son and filled by Your Holy Spirit. I have been washed and raised up. I am walking in newness of life!

Let Thy hand be upon the man of Thy right hand,

upon the son of the man

whom Thou didst make strong for Thyself.

Then we shall not turn back from Thee;

revive us, and we will call upon Thy name.

O Lord God of hosts, restore us;

cause Thy face to shine upon us,

and we will be saved.

--Psalm 80:17-19

Day 358

3/29/16

It has been 432 days since I left home because the man I was married to broke our marriage. And today I've had the breakthrough of all times.

If I realize, believe, and admit what "he" has done, I will have to believe and admit that I am bad because I picked "him!" But the truth is Lord, "my picker" was bad! I had no idea how to pick a husband! And I had no idea what kind of husband You would choose. I was just living for myself!

But, You, Lord, You worked in me during my entire married life to bring me here. You brought me to see my roots grow deep down into You. Thank You, Lord! And You are leading me and showing me which direction to go now.

Lead me in Thy truth and teach me,

for Thou art the God of my salvation;

for Thee I wait all the day.

--Psalm 25:5

Day 359

6/30/16

Oh Dear Lord, what do You want of my life now? I'm searching for new direction. I want my life to count for something, but what will that be! Will it be enough for me to just put one day in front of the other?

Thank You, Lord, for the special life You have planned might just be for me to walk daily with You.

How blessed is the man who does not walk in the counsel of the wicked,

nor stand in the path of sinners,

nor sit in the seat of scoffers.

But his delight is in the law of the Lord,

and in His law he meditates day and night.

And he will be like a tree firmly planted by streams of water,

which yields fruit in its season,

and its leaf does not wither;

and in whatever he does, he prospers.

--Psalm 1:1-3

Day 360

6/27/15

Knowing You, Lord, is the most important thing! Sharing You with others and encouraging others with Your truth is amazing! Lord, it's so wonderful to finally get a breath of fresh air, even through the tears!

Thank You, Lord, that I can now understand and walk in the truth that You are with me each moment! You are building Your word, Your truths, and principles into my life for me to share with others.

He who did not spare His own Son,

but delivered Him over for us all,

how will He not also with Him freely give us all things?

--Romans 8:32

Day 361

12/29/16

Wow, I just survived days and days of Christmas movies—months, really! Almost all of them center on a romantic theme. As I was watching them, I kept thinking: "Why am I obsessing over these movies where the girl always gets the guy and visa-versa?" Am I missing the whole point of Christmas?

My only conclusion is that they are really about hope. And that is what Christmas is about, the hope that Jesus brought into the fallen world. I can really appreciate that!

I have hoped a lot this year. I have hoped that God would show me what to do. I have hoped that He would keep me safe even in troubling times. I hoped that He would meet my needs and love me. And He has shown Himself real to me this year!

I suppose it's what we are all looking for, something to pin our hopes on! I choose the Baby who was born in a stable and laid in a manger for me and you!

But the angel said to them,

"Do not be afraid; for behold,

I bring you good news of great joy which will be for all the people;

for today in the city of David there has been born for you a Savior,

who is Christ the Lord.

This will be a sign for you:

you will find a baby wrapped in cloths and

lying in a manger.

And suddenly there appeared with the angel a multitude

of the heavenly host praising God and saying,

"Glory to God in the highest,

*and on earth peace among men
with whom He is pleased."*

--Luke 2:10-14

Day 362

9/17/15

Excerpt from my journal, Day 1 minus 362 (written almost a year before Day 1):

"I keep seeing in this phrase… Let your heart take courage…as if it is an act to do, as if courage is there all along to be picked up and laid down!"

How great is Thy goodness,

which Thou hast stored up for those who fear Thee,

which Thou hast wrought for those who take refuge in Thee,

before the sons of men!

--Psalm 31:19

Thank You, Lord; You are with us. You are always ready to bestow upon us Your great peace and care. And we can take courage through our everyday happenings! We love You, Lord!

Day 363

4/14/16

I'm nearing the end of a very long journey--a journey I never wanted or dreamed about! But the transformation in my heart and life because of the journey has been amazing.

Three years ago when I first suspected that my husband was leaving our marriage, I was a mess of fear and doubt. I was tossed about by every emotion. And I was filled with "what ifs." I was lost in the pain of deceit and lies and confusion. I was overwhelmed and angry!

Because I knew Jesus, I began the work of trusting Him with each moment of my life. I could not have survived this far without Him. He is my God!

When I met a thought or emotion, I practiced crying out to Him. And He continually showed me His strong arms which hold me up. He is my protector.

This has been a tough journey; Thank You, Lord!

Rule #7   God's arm is long enough to walk with me every step. God loves!

Know that the Lord Himself is God;

it is He who has made us,

and not we ourselves;

we are His people

and the sheep of His pasture.

--Psalm 110:3

Day 364

7/9/16

I think I may have finally stopped counting!

I've lived through grief and sorrow before--when my mom died suddenly. And when my dad was taken by insidious dementia. After those times I counted: one month, six months, one year, and two years, until it began to get far away.

But this grief has carried on as if alive with no rhyme and no foreseeable reason. And now the days are too many to even think!

Until tonight--I had an entire conversation and didn't mention my pain at all! I didn't have a thought of it. Maybe I've stopped counting the days since I left my life behind.

Thank You, Lord; You have helped me though this terrible grief. You have counted each day. You are carrying me to the other side. I cannot understand it, but I can know that You will use this present and the past grief to change me! I can face the days one by one with You!

Thine eyes have seen my unformed substance;

and in Thy book they were all written,

the days that were ordained for me,

when as yet there was not one of them.

--Psalm 139:16

Day 365

1/20/16

I hope that in these pages you have seen hope and joy and thankfulness. This has been my intent. And I hope you have seen the truth that God loves you and me, for this is my dream. May we each know, no matter what, God is with us. He wants the highest and best good for our lives. And that even in our most difficult circumstances, God's grace will come shining through on us!

I know that in the midst of some of the hard things and because we've been through them, we can see more clearly! Because it is true that in the darkness, a great light shines. Knowing that we can endure these difficulties while walking with the Lord is life changing!

This contrast of the light in the darkness can give courage to a friend. It can remind us that God has not blinked. He has endured with us and even gone before us.

Thank You, Lord, for these words to share. Thank You for the pain before the words. Thank You for the longing to know You more! Thank You for the comfort and courage and for Your sweet love!

I will sing of the lovingkindness of the Lord forever;

to all generations I will make known

Thy faithfulness with my mouth.

--Psalm 89:1

Day 366

10/17/16

Oh my, it has been 600 days since I left my house. It finally seems so very far away. There is a new layer of space between my life then and my life now! WOW!

This week I felt the fight coming back into me. When I realized that it was over 600 days, something changed in my heart. I'm really ready to fight for my new life.

I think that up until now I've been saying, "Thank You, Lord," to build a habit. Sometimes I would connect with the thankfulness, but sometimes I just said it on purpose. But now I can see that this Thankful Journey is not a default life. This is my life which is chosen by God. This is my planned life; it is planned by Him! I don't need to think of it as if my life were derailed by my husband's deceit. I can think of it as Redeemed. I have a life redeemed by God!

Thank You, Lord, for redeeming me and my life! Thank You for being big and greater than all our sin! I love You, Lord.

For the grace of God has appeared,

bringing salvation to all men,

instructing us to deny ungodliness and worldly desires

and to live sensibly, righteously and godly in the present age,

looking for the blessed hope

and the appearing of the glory

of our great God and Savior, Christ Jesus,

who gave Himself for us to redeem us from every lawless deed,

and to purify for Himself a people for His own possession,

zealous for good deeds.

These things speak and exhort and reprove with all authority.

Let no one disregard you.

--Titus 2:11-15

Day 367

9/9/16

The next step...today a friend is coming to begin proofreading the book. Dear Lord, please let Your words and Your heart go forward. Keep me out of the way!

I am so utterly frightened, thinking of this book getting out there into the world. But isn't that why You had me write all these things down?

Thank You, Lord; these are thoughts from You and scriptures from Your word! Send them to the right eyes, ears and hearts. Please let them comfort and heal!

And the Lord will continually guide you

and satisfy your desire in scorched places,

and give strength to your bones;

and you will be like a watered garden,

and like a spring of water whose waters do not fail.

--Isaiah 58:11

Day Horrible--368

12/3/16

Today I found out that "he" filed for a marriage license! Even after everything I've been through, I was still shocked! I guess nothing can really prepare you to hear that the person you gave your heart to is marrying someone else!

But then I realized that I had been praying and asking God to close the door. That license finally closes the door. I can say "It's done." In fact, it closes so many doors such as: "If only I had done this or that." And it puts so many things in perspective from the past three or four years.

So I guess that December 3, 2016, is not a horrible day after all. It is in fact a victory day! Thank You, Lord, for the victory. I'm walking with You and not turning back!

Sing to the Lord a new song,

for He has done wonderful things,

His right hand and His holy arm have gained victory for Him.

The Lord has made known His salvation;

He has revealed His righteousness and His faithfulness

to the house of Israel;

all the ends of the earth have seen the salvation of our God.

Shout joyfully to the Lord,

all the earth;

break forth and sing for joy and sing praises.

--Psalm 98:1-4

Day 369

12/7/16

I wish I could say that I know I've cried my last tear. I wish I could tell you that there won't be any more pain and that you will only feel happy from now on. And that you'll never look back again. I wish we would never wonder why and never question God again. I'm not going to say these things because they are just not true.

The truth is, going forward from here, we all have a journey to walk with the Lord. It's a moment by moment clinging to Him, no matter what bad stuff has happened to us. No matter how painful our lives are, we still get to walk with the Lord every day. And that really is the whole point…walking with the Lord.

I'm writing this with tears running down my face, but its okay. God's arm is long enough to hold me today.

Rule #7 God's arm is long enough to walk with me every step. God loves!

Sing praises to the Lord,

who dwells in Zion;

declare among the peoples His deeds.

For He who requires blood remembers them;

He does not forget the cry of the afflicted.

Be gracious to me, O Lord;

behold my affliction from those who hate me,

Thou who dost lift me up from the gates of death;

that I may tell of all Thy praises,

that in the gates of the daughter of Zion

I may rejoice in Thy salvation.

--Psalm 9:11-14

Day 370

2/16/17

I have talked a lot about closing the door. I have felt that, at some point, a feeling of finality would come to me. This would mean that I could stop looking back, stop thinking about "it" and "him." You and I both know this will not happen, at least not in the way we imagine.

I realize that because this is all wrapped up in grief, it will trail along behind me. It seems that pain is so intricately connected with joy and hope that it cannot ever be fully separated! There will be times, which begin to stretch out longer, when I don't think about it. And the little darty thoughts of remembering the relationship and the pain will not come so often. I will find more times of stepping into my life on purpose instead of just coasting along to get through it. And I will be able to stop holding everything up against the past few years. Maybe I will not have to think so much about what I have lost! But I will keep looking forward with hope for all God can do with my life!

Thank You, Lord, for walking me through this season. Thank You for Your great wisdom in directing my life. Please keep reminding me to lay aside the dwelling on my past and pick up each new day. Your days are precious.

I will hear what God the Lord will say;

For He will speak peace to His people, His godly ones;

but let them not turn back to folly.

Surely His salvation is near to those who fear Him,

that glory may dwell in our land.

Lovingkindness and truth have met together;

righteousness and peace have kissed each other.

Truth springs from the earth,

and righteousness looks down from heaven.

the Lord will give what is good, and our land will yield its produce.

Righteousness will go before Him and will make His footsteps into a way.

--Psalm 85:8-13

THE BEGINNING...